Mike Aquilina

The World of Ben-Hur

SOPHIA INSTITUTE PRESS
Manchester, New Hampshire

Visit the motion picture website at www.benhurmovie.com.

Cover design by Perceptions Design Studio.

Sophia Institute Press
Box 5284, Manchester, NH 03108
1-800-888-9344

www.SophiaInstitute.com

Library of Congress Cataloging-in-Publication Data

Names: Aquilina, Mike, author.
Title: The world of Ben-Hur / Mike Aquilina.
Description: Manchester, New Hampshire : Sophia Institute Press, 2016. | Includes bibliographical references.
Identifiers: LCCN 2016011150 | ISBN 9781622823178 (pbk. : alk. paper)
Subjects: LCSH: Wallace, Lew, 1827-1905. Ben-Hur. | Wallace, Lew, 1827-1905. | Christianity in literature. | Authors, American—19th century—Biography. | Literature and society—United States—History—19th century.
Classification: LCC PS3134 .B427 2016 | DDC 813/.4 [B] —dc23 LC record available at https://lccn.loc.gov/2016011150

First printing

To my sister Mary

Contents

The World of Ben-Hur

1

The Life-Changing Encounter with History

Who cares about history?

The hardest thing to explain to any high school student is why we should care about history. You can make a case for science. You can explain the use of geometry. You might even be able to prove that Nathaniel Hawthorne is worth something. But history? Come on. Who cares what happened in 54 B.C.?

But take those same teenagers out of the high school, and you'll find that they *do* care, very deeply. The proof of it is that we have another movie version of *Ben-Hur*.

People naturally want to feel a connection with the past. It almost seems to be coded into our DNA. Long before writing was invented, we were telling stories about our origins, our ancient heroes, and our family history. We sat around the campfire, listening to the oldest member of the tribe tell us what he had heard from his great-grandmother, and we were enthralled. The distant past came alive in our imaginations.

And in that imaginary encounter with the past, we learned about ourselves. We learned why we believed what we believed, why we did what we did, how we got to be where we are now. Instinctively we knew then, and we know now, that the answers to our questions about the present all lie somewhere in the past.

Christians have always been especially attracted to that encounter with the past in the imagination, because our religion is based on a historical event. A particular thing happened in a particular place at a particular time, and it changed everything: that's what Christians believe. We believe that our lives are fundamentally different today because of things that happened in Jerusalem in the first century.

How do we encounter that history? How do we make it *live*, so that we feel as though we've experienced it, not just heard some dry facts about it?

First, we can read the original sources. There are four histories of Jesus' life—the Gospels. There's a history of the very beginning of the Church—the Acts of the Apostles. We also get some glimpses of the world of the early Christians from the letters they wrote, especially the letters of Paul.

But for modern readers many of those sources are not as vivid as they were a couple of millennia ago. The Gospels tell us the facts, but they are very sparing with the atmosphere. That's not surprising. The Gospels were originally written by and for people who lived in the same world Jesus lived in.

Think of all the things you take for granted when you read or write about the world today. If you say "Manhattan" in an American book, that's all you have to say to bring up images of a crowded island bristling with skyscrapers, filled with millions of people from every continent, loud with the noises of traffic jams and subway trains. Even an American who has never been to New York can *imagine* Manhattan. So it was in the first century: if you said "Antioch" or "Jerusalem," that was all you had to say to fill people's minds with images, sounds, smells, and ideas. The New Testament writers took that background for granted and concentrated on the message that people *hadn't* heard.

When you think about it, that probably explains something about the extraordinarily rapid spread of Christianity in those first few centuries. Here was a riveting story that people could imagine happening right in front of their eyes. It was real, and it had happened in their own world. They could see the sights, hear the sounds, smell the smells.

It wasn't until that world disappeared that people needed a little help imagining the world of Christ and the apostles.

In the Middle Ages, most people in Europe couldn't read. Even for the people who could read, books were rare—and thus extraordinarily valuable. Great churches or monasteries had libraries where the books were chained to desks.

Yet Christianity, as we remember, is a historical religion. It's based entirely on the fact that certain things happened at particular times in history. So how do you teach people sacred history when they can't read? And how do you get them to care? How do you make the events vivid to them, when the world is utterly different from the way it was when those events happened?

The answer medieval Europeans came up with was the mystery plays.

You could gather people into churches and preach at them, but—as many a modern preacher has found—you can't really make them listen. But if you actually show them the stories, they perk up. They pay attention. They remember the message.

It started in the churches, with just a little bit of illustrative acting out of the stories. After a while, the acting out grew into full-scale dramas with scripts and characters. When the Church authorities decided that priests should not take part in stage plays, the guilds—associations of craftsmen—took over the management of the plays. After that, they grew into huge events that the whole town turned out to see, with elaborate costumes and props to make the whole experience feel all the more real.

The anonymous writers of these plays—probably monks at first—approached their subjects with great freedom. You could say they had a lot of fun with them. They peered behind the scenes in the Gospel stories, imagining what was really going on, just as movies like *Ben-Hur* do today.

Here's a good example. We know the story of the woman taken in adultery (John 8:1-11). The scribes and Pharisees brought to Jesus a woman who had been caught in adultery and asked what should be done with her. It was a test: they knew Jesus' forgiving nature, but they knew that the Law said she should be stoned. And they knew the Romans didn't allow them to stone people for adultery. One way or another, they were going to catch him. And Jesus caught them instead, making them ashamed of themselves by telling them, "Let him who is without sin among you be the first to throw a stone at her."

It's a good story, but how did it start? Who is this woman? How did she get caught?

One of those old mystery plays takes us back to the beginning. It introduces a representative scribe character and a representative Pharisee character, both complaining about how this hypocritical Jesus character—son of a shepherd's daughter!—is leading the people away from the Law. Oh, if only we could cook up some scheme to make the people turn against him! And then along comes an accuser who tells them he has just the thing. There's a case of adultery going on *right now*. We can catch them in the act! Then if that Jesus fellow still preaches mercy, we've got him!

We get to see the scribe and Pharisee gleefully plotting. We laugh at the young woman's lover running away, still pulling his pants up. We see the woman begging the scribe and Pharisee for mercy, offering them bribes, and finally begging them to kill her quietly rather than shame her in public. We see them bring her to Jesus, and we watch as Jesus writes in the dirt. And we find out *what* he was writing in the dirt: he was listing all the sins of the scribe, the Pharisee, and the accuser. The whole story comes alive in front of the whole town. The people go home and feel as if they *know* those characters. They have seen history. They met Jesus; they knew that woman; they saw the scribe and the Pharisee. They will never forget that story. It will live in their imaginations forever.

We could call this *devotional fiction*. The main characters in the story are made up: the Bible doesn't tell us who the woman was, or who the people were who brought her to Jesus, so all those details had to come from the imagination of the playwright. But the fictional characters find themselves actors in a real event, taken from the Gospel. The playwrights are always careful to make sure that nothing they make up contradicts the Bible account. They just fill in details that the audience can relate to. Then, instead of an abstract historical event, the Gospel story becomes real in their imaginations. They feel as though they have lived through it themselves.

Purists, of course, might object to the fictional parts of the story. The Bible doesn't tell us any of that stuff about the scheming, about the woman begging, about what Jesus was writing. In England, the Protestants shut down the mystery plays and miracle plays, but the people wouldn't do without their entertainment. If they couldn't have the plays for religious reasons, they would have them in public theaters. The medieval mystery plays led straight to Shakespeare.

The world has changed a lot since medieval times. We have movies, television, and YouTube videos. We don't have to wait for a holy day to come around to enjoy any of them. But human nature hasn't changed. We still want that personal connection with history. We want to go home from the movies feeling as though we were actually there, in ancient Rome. We want the same experience the people of York or Wakefield had centuries ago: not just to *know* what happened, but to *experience* it.

And that's the feeling movies such as *Ben-Hur* are designed to give us.

Picture a comfortably well-off man sitting down to write. He has written a few things before, but as a writer he has been only moderately successful. But now he has what he thinks is a really good plan for a book.

He's fascinated by an idea: the real history of the origins of Christianity hasn't been told. He's not a Christian himself; he has never had any use for religion. But the puzzle of Christian history has gripped him. It's almost as though a great secret has been kept from him, and he's going to find the truth. And then he's going to put it into a popular novel that will be accessible to everybody, because it will have all the action and romance and danger that everybody wants in a novel—but with the added zest of promising to reveal deep secrets about the beginnings of the Christian religion.

Here in the twenty-first century, you're probably picturing Dan Brown. *The Da Vinci Code* was a worldwide publishing sensation, making its author a multimillionaire overnight and dominating every discussion of religion for a year or more after it was published.

But since you're reading about *Ben-Hur*, you might suspect that there's another author who fits this picture. And, of course, you're right. Lew Wallace and Dan Brown both started with that same idea—the idea that you could make a great popular entertainment out of the historical origins of Christianity. And they both succeeded, probably beyond their wildest dreams of success. Dan Brown has sold more than two hundred million copies of his books. And *Ben-Hur: A Tale of the Christ* was the best-selling American book of the entire nineteenth century. It broke the record long held by *Uncle Tom's Cabin*, and its own record wouldn't be broken until *Gone with the Wind*—fifty years later.

The stories of these two publishing sensations are similar—surprisingly similar, when you think about how different the times were. *Ben-Hur* was published in 1880; *The Da Vinci Code* was published in 2003. A lot happened in those 123 years. But one thing hadn't changed: people had an aching need to see into the past, to know what really happened at the beginning of Christianity. This is what we all want. We want to be there, to see the sights, hear the sounds, even smell the smells. We want to feel what it was like to be alive when the Christian religion was something new.

When *The Da Vinci Code* was published, literary critics dismissed it. They said the characters were wooden. The dialogue was implausible. Characters marched on stage just to explain something and then marched off again. The plot was contrived; it depended on ridiculous coincidences. The book was badly written, a museum of failed sentences. It "gives bad novels a bad name," said Salman Rushdie.

But influential celebrities picked it up and ran with it. They thought it was the most exciting thing they had ever read. It told them things about history they had never known before. And it didn't really matter that those things were *wrong;* it *felt* as though history were opening up and revealing its secrets.

The story was a formulaic thriller, designed to keep pages turning with short chapters and a cliffhanger at the end of each chapter. But it was not the thriller part of the story that captured people. Dan Brown had written three thrillers before that one, all with more or less the same structure. It was the *ideas* that made *The Da Vinci Code* a worldwide phenomenon. People felt as though they were learning *what really happened* for the first time. Reputable historians might publish long gray refutations of Dan Brown's supposed history, but no one paid any attention to reputable historians. Could reputable historians give them something as much fun as a two-thousand-year-old conspiracy protected by albino Opus Dei assassins?

Let's flash back to 1880, and we'll find ourselves in almost the same world. *Ben-Hur* was dismissed by the literary critics of the day. They said the characters were wooden. The dialogue was implausible. Characters marched on stage just to explain something and then marched off again. The plot was contrived; it depended on ridiculous coincidences. But the celebrities of the day latched on to the book and wouldn't let go.

Ulysses S. Grant, former president and the general who won the Civil War, was a huge fan. So was Jefferson Davis, the former president of the Confederacy. The word began to circulate that here was a book that made the time of Christ alive. You could see the sights, hear the sounds, smell the smells.

Preachers started to recommend it to their flocks. Sunday schools started to read it in groups. President Garfield was such a big fan, and so impressed by the minute descriptions of Eastern life, that he sent Wallace to Constantinople as the United

States' minister to the Ottoman Empire (which governed the Holy Land in those days). Taking advantage of the publicity, the publishers brought out a luxurious thirty-dollar "Garfield Edition" of *Ben-Hur*, complete with Garfield's own fan letter to Wallace as an introduction. The average laborer might be happy to make thirty dollars in a month, but there were people who spent that on a copy of *Ben-Hur*.

As time went on, *Ben-Hur* went from success to success. It made its author rich; it was published in cheap editions for the mass market and luxury editions for the parlors of the rich. It was adapted into a stage play, with real horses thundering on a giant treadmill for the chariot race. It toured the great cities of America and was a smash in London as well.

In 1907, it was made into a one-reel movie, less than fifteen minutes long, with some of the cast from the stage show. (American movie producers were still clinging to the idea that no one would sit still for a subject that took up more than one reel.) The chariot race used borrowed firemen's horses on a beach, with the firemen themselves driving the chariots: they go past the stationary camera while a few extras cheer, and then they do it again, and again, until finally a title card declares, "BEN HUR VICTOR," and we see Judah being congratulated. It was a very simple production, but by the standards of the time it was thrilling.

This movie is an interesting footnote in history: like almost all American movies in those early days, it was done without paying for any rights to the story. Early movie producers looked on any story as fair game, and there simply was no case law on the subject. But the publisher of the book sued, and the court case set the important precedent that movies have to abide by the same copyright rules as everybody else. It was *Ben-Hur* that was responsible for establishing the principle that you do actually have to ask the author of a novel before you make his story into a movie.

In 1925 the story was made into a blockbuster movie. This time, the Wallace estate got its cut. And in those eighteen years, the movies had made enormous progress. Now they were capable of almost any illusion: the 1925 version brings the whole world of ancient Rome to life. In a stage show, the production was limited by the size of the theater. By 1925 the movies had almost no limits, because the movie could make you believe anything the camera could trick your eye into seeing.

The chariot race in the 1925 movie is still one of the most famous scenes in the history of the movies. The movie had what was, for the time, a colossal budget of nearly four million dollars, making it the most expensive movie of the whole silent era. Moviegoers were astonished to see an entire Roman circus built on the most lavish scale for the chariot race. It was one of the most-talked-about scenes in history. And it all depended on a clever visual trick that was kept secret for decades after the film was released.

There was no way MGM—a new studio—could afford to build an entire Roman circus, even on *Ben-Hur*'s budget. Instead, the set designers built stands for the lower part of the audience and filled them with extras. For the upper part of the set, with all its magnificent architectural flourishes, a miniature model was constructed, complete with little wooden people who could be moved up and down as the audience jumped up to cheer. With the optical geometry calculated to the last inch, the wooden model was hung in front of the camera so that it perfectly completed the stands filled with extras. Even today, it's almost impossible for the most attentive viewer to see where the set ends and the model begins.

That's what a movie can do for us: it gives us the feeling that we were really there, that we really saw what it was like to be in a Roman circus. It gives us that feeling of *owning* the past that the people of York felt when they watched their mystery plays, but magnified by the ability of the movies to let us see almost anything we want to see. No wonder the 1925 movie was the biggest blockbuster of the whole silent era.

When MGM made *Ben-Hur* with sound and color in 1959, the studio knew better than to meddle with success. The 1959 chariot race duplicates almost exactly, shot for shot, the 1925 version. And *Ben-Hur* was an even bigger hit in 1959 than it had been in 1925.

That chariot race, incidentally, is one of the defining moments of the movies, one of the most imitated scenes in history. You'll recognize it even in a galaxy far, far away, where it was the obvious inspiration for the pod race in *Star Wars Episode I: The Phantom Menace*.

Dan Brown and Lew Wallace both promised us glimpses into the origins of Christianity. And we lined up around the block for both of them. But what did they believe personally?

Neither writer was a Christian when he started his blockbuster novel. Lew Wallace was an agnostic—he had no religious faith. Dan Brown was raised an Episcopalian but drifted away when he rejected a fundamentalist interpretation of the Bible.[1] Even so, there's a big difference between the two books. *Ben-Hur*

1 "Dan Brown: 'Science Makes More Sense to Me," interview with James Kaplan, *Parade*, September 14, 2009, archived at Today Books, retrieved August 2, 2015, www.today.com.

takes as its starting assumption the idea that the Bible stories are true, at least as historical narratives; *The Da Vinci Code* assumes that they are false, and the real truth has been hidden from us.

In spite of that difference, they do have this in common: they promise us an insight into history we haven't been able to get anywhere else. One of them actually delivers on that promise.

It's that same problem the people of medieval Europe faced. The world of the Roman Empire has disappeared, and the Gospel stories don't give us enough details to reconstruct it in our imaginations. Yet something tells us we're not getting the message if we don't have a picture of the world in our minds. St. Josemaría Escríva believed that a strong mental picture of the world of the Gospels was essential to understanding the message:

> I advised you to read the New Testament and to enter into each scene and take part in it, as one more of the characters. The minutes you spend in this way each day enable you to incarnate the Gospel, reflect it in your life and help others to reflect it.[2]

This was exactly what *Ben-Hur* gave its legions of readers, and later the even larger numbers of people who would see it in the various movie versions. Lew Wallace almost unconsciously hit on exactly the right way to make the Jesus story come alive so that we could live *in* it, not just hear it or see it.

He could have written a novelized version of the Acts of the Apostles, or followed one of the other biblical characters through his semifictional life. Others have tried that and had some success.

[2] Josemaría Escríva, *Furrow* (New York: Scepter Publishers, 2002), no. 672.

But by creating these fictional characters and putting them in the real story of Christ and first-century Judea, he makes us realize what a big world it was. Any one of us could have been in that world—in Jerusalem, in Rome, in Antioch. There's room for us there. There's room for us to experience the sights, sounds, and smells of Jerusalem and Antioch as they were in those days. There's room for us to mingle with the crowds as they gather around the carpenter who has started to preach a revolution of peace. There's room for us at the foot of the Cross.

That's what we want. We want to *know what it was like*.

We want to enjoy that grand spectacle of ancient Rome. We want to see the shocking violence and immorality that was constantly on display—but we also want to see it repudiated by the end of the movie, because it leaves us feeling sick if good doesn't prevail.

That's what stories like *Ben-Hur* give us. They let us see the sights and hear the sounds of those distant days of Roman glory. But they also show us that the glory died for a good reason, and that the Christian civilization that replaced it was better. By the end of the movie, we can be back home where we belong. We can have our gladiators and chariot races, but we can also be happy to live in a world where the things we see happening in ancient Rome aren't allowed—not even in NASCAR.

And that's why blockbuster movies, just like best-selling novels, are always returning to Christian origins. They give us a sense that *we were there*—that we actually saw the beginnings of the Christian movement, that we knew what it was like to follow Christ down the Via Dolorosa.

Sometimes they get their history right. Sometimes they get it wrong. But if they lure us into history at all, they're doing a good thing. Once we get started down that road, we may actually learn what really happened. And then, like Lew Wallace, we'll have no choice but to believe. Because that's what happened to him. And the story of *how* it happened is almost as interesting as his novel is.

2

The Man Who Dreamed Ben-Hur

"My God! Did I set all this in motion?"

Lew Wallace was taking a behind-the-scenes tour of the *Ben-Hur* stage show, soon to open in New York. The centerpiece of the whole show was the chariot race, which is hard enough to stage for a movie, so you can imagine how it was for a live show. In this case, there were real horses running on a cleverly designed treadmill, with scenery rolling past in the background.

As Wallace looked around, he simply couldn't believe how much money was being spent, how many people were working day after day—all to bring the story he dreamed up to life.

Like the book, the show had critics holding their noses. And like the book, it was a sensational hit. People couldn't stop talking about that chariot race.

It amazed Lew Wallace to see the preparations for a stage version of his novel. What would he have said if he could have seen the titanic effort that goes into making a Hollywood epic?

Tens of millions of dollars go into making a movie like *Ben-Hur*. Thousands of people spend months, sometimes years, making a story that will appear on the movie screen for two hours or so.

And Lew Wallace set it all in motion. One man with a pen dipped in purple ink.

Who was this Lew Wallace, anyway?
Flash back to 1862.

❧

It's the bloodiest battle of the Civil War so far—Shiloh, a name that will live on in the history as a representative bloodbath. General Grant is in bad shape: his horse fell on him a few days ago, and he can't walk without crutches. The Confederate forces have pushed Grant's men back to the river. He needs reinforcements.

Where is General Wallace?

That was the question that would haunt Lew Wallace's career for the rest of his life. Where was General Lew Wallace when Grant needed him at Shiloh?

The answer was that he was on his way to where he thought Grant was, but Grant had moved. Grant insisted that he had sent Wallace orders to go by one road; Wallace insisted that he never got those orders. He was taking another road—one that would have led his little force right into the back of the Confederate army. A messenger caught up with him at last, and Wallace turned around. But he and his men had missed much of the worst of the battle. When they did arrive, they were exhausted from a long roundabout march.

Grant was very annoyed, to say the least. For years afterward, he insisted that Wallace had disobeyed his orders. It was not until 1885 that Grant learned a little more about the circumstances: a letter Wallace had written before the battle finally came to light, detailing his plans for joining Grant at Shiloh. That changed Grant's mind. But the only effect on history was a footnote in Grant's memoirs saying that he wouldn't think the same way now. Who reads footnotes?

It was all the more irksome for Wallace because he had never wanted to be anything other than a great soldier. In his old age, he remembered back to his school days in the 1830s and a sight that gave him a lifelong love of the military life.

> About that time—at least, while my first school engagement lasted—the Black Hawk War was in occurrence, and a company of horsemen formed in Covington to go out after the ferocious chief. The excitement ran high, and culminated the day the volunteers packed their saddle-bags with crackers and cheese, swung their firearms to their backs, and in files of two rode away amid the tears of wives and mothers. There was no school, to be sure, while that scene was enacting, and I saw it all, and was filled with it. Thereafter my hours in the contracted academy were divided between making pictures and fighting battles on my paper slate.[3]

From then on, soldiers and battles were all he thought of. His delight in them led him straight into history, of course, and Wallace remembered a summer spent with his brother William and their playmates reenacting the famous battles of Scottish history as they were described in a historical novel by Jane Porter.

> Each took a character. On account of his name my brother's right to the role of Sir William [the hero of the novel] was admitted. Evans took Robert Bruce; Rawles and Harper had their parts; and I was given the role of the youthful brother of the love-lorn Helen Mar. Then,

[3] Lew Wallace, *An Autobiography*, vol. 1 (New York: Harper and Brothers, 1906), 21-22.

> in deadliest earnest, we went to war with the haughty English. We made helmets of pasteboard and swords of seasoned clapboards. The young hazel-shoots we wove into shields. Our steeds we found ready in the bottom, and that they were of ironweeds did not detract from their fitness. Under us they had the endurance of Arabs and the strength of the big Flemings so affected by knights who ate, drank, and slept in steel. Neither did we see any inconsistency in converting the same weeds into lances. Thus armed and panoplied we ranged the country round. Woe to the elder, the mullen, and the white-crowned lobelias. Woe particularly to the wild sunflower cropping myriadly in the dry hollows under the trees along the river-bank. A vigorous growth of fruiting pokeberries was an enemy to be dealt with in single combat. The sword was then the preferred weapon. Out rode Sir William or the Bruce, and they always came back victorious, their blades dyed to the hilt, their shields dripping with gore.

This was the man who was hoping for glory in the War between the States. Instead, his reputation as a soldier was tarnished forever, and not even considerable heroism later in the war could save it. He returned to active duty in 1864 and was credited by Grant with saving Washington from Confederate invasion.

We shouldn't pity Wallace too much. His military career was seriously damaged by the incident, but he was still a general. After the war, he continued to do useful work, practicing law, meddling a bit in politics—and writing, which he did to relieve the boredom of practicing law. He never really liked practicing law.

Wallace's first novel was a historical epic called *The Fair God*, set during the Spanish conquest of Mexico. It was moderately successful—enough to allow him the luxury of thinking himself a successful novelist, but not enough to allow him the luxury of giving up his day job. He had spent years researching the subject: he found that each incident, each setting, and each character in the story led him back to the libraries to find out more about what Mexico was like in the time of the conquistadors.

This was a habit that would serve him well when he came to write his next novel.

What got Lew Wallace started on writing "a tale of the Christ"? Actually, it was a conversation with America's most famous atheist.

Robert Ingersoll was everyone's favorite crusader against religion. He gave the revival preachers something to shout about. He gave dour New England clergymen a reason to shake their heads in pity. He gave the editors of newspapers something to denounce on a slow news day. And he gave lectures that people paid the enormous sum of a dollar a head to hear, so they could tell their neighbors they had seen the great infidel in person.

He was a large man and a sort of rhetorical steamroller, with an answer for every argument and a mastery of the language that let him dominate every conversation. And one day, when Lew Wallace was riding to Indianapolis on a sleeper train, the great infidel appeared in his nightshirt and said he wanted to talk. He knew General Wallace slightly and knew that Wallace had no use for creeds or churches.

> At that time, speaking candidly, I was not in the least influenced by religious sentiment. I had no convictions

> about God or Christ. I neither believed nor disbelieved in them.
>
> The preachers had made no impression upon me. My reading covered nearly every other subject. Indifference is the word most perfectly descriptive of my feelings respecting the To-morrow of Death, as a French scientist has happily termed the succession of life.

So Ingersoll talked and, as usual, completely dominated the conversation. He trotted out facts—he said they were facts, anyway—in such a rapid and uninterrupted stream that Wallace was completely overwhelmed. And a little ashamed of himself. After all, it hardly seemed right that this famous antireligious crusader should know so much about the origins of Christianity, and Wallace should know nothing, or at least next to nothing. It was obviously an important topic.

For the first time, his indifference to religion struck him as a flaw in his character. He shouldn't be *indifferent*. He should have *certainty*, one way or another. Ingersoll was so certain because he had so much knowledge—at least that was the impression one got from hearing his steamroller rants. So Wallace decided he would have that knowledge too.

How to get it? Immediately he knew the answer to that.

While writing *The Fair God*—a task that took years, on and off—Wallace had made himself an expert on the Spanish conquest of Mexico. Every little point in the narrative, every detail of the backdrop, sent him scurrying back to the books to find out what really happened—how people lived, how they dressed, what they ate, what the climate was like, how they traveled, what they believed.

The lesson was clear to him: if I want to be an expert on something, I need to write a novel about it.

Even in the age of the Internet, researching a historical novel is a daunting task, at least if you want to get the history *right*. You have to know not only where the references are but which ones are useful and which ones will lead you astray (a skill Dan Brown never mastered). You have to take little scraps of evidence and build them into a picture that satisfies the historian on the one hand and makes sense to the ordinary reader on the other.

Now imagine what it was like in the 1800s, with no Internet, no copy machines, no telephones. Public libraries were not thick on the ground: Andrew Carnegie would not donate his first library until three years after the novel *Ben-Hur* was published. Colleges had libraries; there was the Library of Congress; and, of course, there were rich people with private libraries. But how would you even know what was in them? Correspondence had to be sent by letter, or—if you were feeling hurried and had the money—by telegram. Merely chasing down a particular book that *might* tell you what you wanted to know was an adventure.

But Wallace would do that chasing, because he wanted to get the history exactly right. Remember that he wrote the story for the sake of learning the history; he wasn't going to be satisfied with just getting by. He was going to make his historical setting satisfying to the most punctilious historian—in spite of his own obvious limitations.

> In the next place, I had never been to the Holy Land. In making it the location of my story, it was needful not merely to be familiar with its history and geography. I must be able to paint it, water, land, and sky, in actual colors. Nor would the critics excuse me for mistakes in the costumes or customs of any of the peoples representatively

introduced, Greek, Roman, Egyptian, especially the children of Israel.

Ponder the task! There was but one method open to me. I examined catalogues of books and maps, and sent for everything likely to be useful. I wrote with a chart always before my eyes—a German publication, showing the towns and villages, all sacred places, the heights, the depressions, the passes, trails, and distances.

Travellers told me of the birds, animals, vegetation, and seasons. Indeed, I think the necessity for constant reference to authorities saved me mistakes which certainly would have occurred had I trusted to a tourist's memory....

Of the more than seven years given the book, the least part was occupied in actual composition. Research and investigation consumed most of the appropriated time.

I had to be so painstaking! The subject was the one known thoroughly by more scholars and thinkers than any other in the wide range of literature.

After comparing authorities, I had frequently to reconcile them; failing in that, it remained to choose between them. There is nothing, not even a will-o'-the- wisp, so elusive as a disputed date. Once I went to Washington, thence to Boston, for no purpose but to exhaust their libraries in an effort to satisfy myself of the mechanical arrangement of the oars in the interior of a trireme.[4]

To make use of all that research, Wallace dreamed up a story that would take place during the time of Christ. He intended to sell it as a magazine serial—a popular way of publishing novels

[4] Wallace, *An Autobiography*, vol. 2, 932-934.

in the late 1800s. Since he meant to sell it, he had to be careful not to make it offensive to religious readers—which meant that he would have to be very careful about introducing Jesus Christ as a character. He quickly decided that Christ couldn't be the *main* character. Instead, his story would be about someone who lived at the same time as Christ, and how Christ's presence on earth affected that person.

> My characters are essentially living persons. They arise and sit, look, talk, and behave like themselves.
>
> In dealing with them I see them; when they speak I hear them. I know them by their features. They answer my call. Some of them I detest. Such as I most affect become my familiars. In turn they call me, and I recognize their voices.

Some literary critics might dispute the "living" quality of Lew Wallace's characters. To many readers they seem wooden, like puppets made to clatter across the stage for the purpose of making the point the author has in mind. But there is no question that they occupied his imagination. As he told their story, he filled in more and more of the world behind them. And as the world filled in, Wallace found himself inevitably led down a surprising path toward a destination he had not expected. In fact, he was finding his certainty. The more he wrote, the more he got to know his characters—both the imagined ones and the historical ones with whom they interacted.

> Such being the case, think of the society to which the serial directly admitted me!
>
> Think of riding with Balthasar on his great white camel to the meeting appointed beyond Moab; of

association with the mysterious Three [Wise Men]; of breaking fast with them in the shade of the little tent pitched on the rippled sand; of hearing the "grace" with which they began their repast; of listening as they introduced themselves to one another, telling how and when and where they were severally summoned by the Spirit; of the further guestship in the final journey to Jerusalem, the star our guide!

Think of attending a session of the Sanhedrin; of hearing Herod the Builder ask Hillel, more than a hundred years a scholar, where the new King of the Jews was most likely to be discovered!

Think of lying with the shepherds in their sheepfold that clear, crisp, first Christmas night; of seeing the ladder of light drop out of the window of heaven; of hearing the Annunciator make proclamation of his glad tidings!

Think of walking with Joseph from the Joppa gate across the plain of Rephaim, past the tomb of Rachel, up to the old khan by Bethlehem; of stealing glances at the face of the girl-wife on the donkey, she who was so shortly to be, in good old Catholic phrase, the Blessed Mother of God!

Think of seeing that face so often and with such distinctness as to be able to pronounce that there are but two portraits of her in the world, Raphael's and Murillo's, all the others being either too old, too vulgar, or too human! Then tell me, was it strange if I wrote reverentially, and sometimes with awe? Or that I was unconsciously making ready to cast my indifference as a locust casts its shell?[5]

[5] Ibid., 928-929.

The indifference was fading. The famous atheist Ingersoll had given him the first shove, and Wallace spent years on his journey of discovery. He was rather surprised to find out where he had ended up.

> As this article is in the nature of confessions, here is one which the reader may excuse, and at the same time accept as a fitting conclusion: Long before I was through with my book, I became a believer in God and Christ.

By finding out as much as he could about the real history of the time of Christ, Wallace became a Christian convert. He never joined a church: to the end of his life, Wallace was not so much hostile as indifferent to organized religion. But he was certain that Jesus Christ was divine. The history had convinced him of it.

> I am not a member of any church or denomination, nor have I ever been. Not that churches are objectionable to me, but simply because my freedom is enjoyable, and I do not think myself good enough to be a communicant. None the less I believe in the Divinity of Jesus Christ.[6]

As we already know, *Ben-Hur: A Tale of the Christ* was a great success. Not at first, though. It attracted little attention when it was first published, and the reviews were mixed at best. But word of mouth, and a few lucky celebrity endorsements, made the difference: the book started to take off. In a few years, Wallace had made enough money to retire very comfortably. In fact, by most standards, he was rich. He used some of the money to build himself a curious Byzantine study from his own plans, and

[6] Wallace, *An Autobiography*, vol. 1, 2.

he decorated it with portraits of Judah Ben-Hur and his sister Tirzah. It still stands today as a museum dedicated to the life of the man who dreamed *Ben-Hur.*

Even with all that success, though, Wallace was always a soldier at heart. You may call him intensely patriotic, or you may say that he never stopped being a little boy playing with swords. When the Spanish-American War was declared in 1898, Wallace immediately offered to raise and lead a band of soldiers, but the government had no use for him. So he went to his local recruiting office and tried to enlist as a private. They didn't take him there either. Perhaps they thought seventy-one was a bit old for a private.

As a soldier, Wallace never did get out from under the shadow of Shiloh. In spite of Grant's later retraction, it's most often Grant's earlier story—that Wallace got lost on the way to the battle—that makes it into the history books, even today.

Fortunately for Wallace's reputation, no one remembers him anymore as a failed civil-war general. Everyone remembers him as the blockbuster novelist who gave us *Ben-Hur: A Tale of the Christ.*

3

Conquerors and Philosophers: The Empire That Ruled Ben-Hur

You have to understand the Roman Empire to understand the world of *Ben-Hur*. In fact, you have to understand the Roman Empire to understand the world. Everything Europe is today, and every way in which Europe has affected the rest of the world, depends on the history of Rome and Rome's ideas of government. And certainly the whole story of *Ben-Hur* depends on the empire and the way it dealt with its conquered provinces.

Rome began as a little town in Italy, one of hundreds or thousands. No one would have thought it was anything worth mentioning in the what-to-see-in-Italy brochure. If you had looked at Italy from outside in about 700 B.C., you'd have said that the Etruscans were the ones to watch, or perhaps the thriving Greek colonies in the south.

Greeks had started sending colonies to Italy in the 800s. Italy was the America of the ancient world: a place where ambitious colonists from old Greece dreamed of making fortunes and reputations. Soon southern Italy was mostly Greek, and Greek culture inevitably seeped northward up the peninsula.

Meanwhile, the Etruscans were the big power in northern Italy at the time. We don't know much about them, because although they left written inscriptions, they neglected to leave us an Etruscan dictionary. (The emperor Claudius, who was a much better scholar than he was an emperor, made an Etruscan-to-Latin dictionary by carefully interviewing the last remaining Etruscan speakers, but none of his work has survived.) Roman legend tells us that the Etruscans dominated Italy north of Rome, and archaeology confirms it. For a while the Etruscans dominated Rome itself. Roman historians tell us that Rome threw out her last Etruscan king, Tarquin the Proud, in 509 B.C. His nickname tells you a little about *why* they threw him out.

Once they had thrown out the king, what should they do? Tarquin had made the name of king to stink so badly for the Romans that they never wanted a king again. And in fact they never had another "king" for almost a thousand years after that.

Instead, the Senate—the group of aristocrats who had formerly advised the king—would govern Rome. For those things that required decisive leadership, there would be two consuls elected every year. They had many of the powers of the king, but there were two of them—they had to agree, or nothing got done. And every consul knew he would be gone in a year, so he could not build a permanent power base.

This was a new form of government. What to call it? The Romans, with a simple practicality, called it "the public thing"—*res publica*, later shortened to *republica*. They had invented the republic.

The Roman Republic proved formidable against its enemies. The Romans were always picking fights—and they were always winning them, too. Bit by bit Rome conquered the other cities in Italy. When Rome grew into a regional power, it came into conflict with the Greek colonies in the south of Italy. Rome won that fight, too, absorbing both the Greek colonies and their

Greek culture. Then Carthage, the great North African empire with ambitions to expand across the Mediterranean, became the number-one enemy. It took every ounce of her strength, but Rome defeated Carthage so thoroughly that the city was wiped off the map.

Over the centuries, the Republic grew greater and greater until, after picking fights with nearly everybody in the world, it controlled most of the Mediterranean. It seemed like an unstoppable force.

The one thing that did threaten to stop Rome was not any opposition from outside, but chronic instability inside. The more powerful Rome grew, the more tempting Rome's leading offices were for ruthlessly ambitious politicians. With so many wars going on, successful generals were inevitably the main political figures. Instead of winning the consulship with a clever slogan or two, they were always sorely tempted to fight the election campaign with a massive army. Armies were what they knew. Armies got things done.

Of all these generals, the most successful was Julius Caesar. He expanded Rome's borders like no one before. When he defeated all the other fighting politicians at the end of a bloody civil war, the fawning Senate made him dictator for life.

As it turned out, that was a very short term. As any Shakespeare fan knows, Caesar was assassinated not long into his dictatorship-for-life, and another bloody civil war erupted, one that was fought on a scale hard to imagine. It enveloped most of the Mediterranean world. When the dust and ashes had settled, Octavian, Caesar's adopted son, had defeated everyone else. He took the title Augustus and became the first Roman emperor. Not a king, because Romans didn't have kings: hundreds of years after the last one had been thrown out, *king* was still a bad word in the Roman mouth. It was just that the *res publica* had a new position at the top of the chart. There were still consuls and all the other elective offices, but there was an *imperator* whose word was final.

Suddenly there was peace. Augustus thought that Roman power had been extended far enough: any more would be hard to defend. So there were no big wars of conquest. And Rome was so thoroughly worn out with civil wars that no one seriously challenged Augustus. The *Pax Romana* or Roman Peace, a long period of peace and prosperity throughout the Mediterranean, had begun.

Whatever our own prejudices about emperors, we have to admit that, for the first two centuries at least, the empire worked better than the republic had worked. Civil wars ended, and peace prevailed throughout the Mediterranean. For the first time, it was possible to travel most of the known world unmolested, without crossing a border. The Romans built paved roads everywhere, so land travel was faster and safer than ever before. And having defeated his other enemies, Augustus was free to make the seas safe as well by tackling the piracy problem. (You'll remember the piracy problem popping up for a while in *Ben-Hur*.)

If ever there were a perfect time for one single idea to spread from Asia through Europe and Africa, this was it.

And in the reign of Caesar Augustus, Jesus Christ was born in Bethlehem.

The powerful Roman military was what held this sprawling empire together. The Romans discouraged regional loyalties among the soldiers by sending soldiers across the empire to places they had never seen before. One of the legions patrolling far-off Britain, for example, was the Ninth Spanish Legion, so called because it had fought in Spain before being shipped off to patrol the very northern frontier of the empire.

The Roman army was made up mostly of Roman citizens in those days. In the later centuries of the empire, "barbarian" mercenaries—foreigners from outside the empire lured by the high pay—would make up most of the army, but the armies that conquered the world and kept the Roman Peace were Roman.

In some ways, the Roman army of the first century was much like today's American army. Discipline was harsher, to be sure. But it was a professional organization, the best armed force in the world. It treated soldiers as valuable, and it took care of them when they retired. It recognized talent, too: a man who started from nothing might rise through the ranks if he showed enthusiasm and intelligence. So it was a good career choice for someone like *Ben-Hur*'s Messala, who had education and background but nothing else to his name. If he survived to retire, he might retire with a nice plot of land and a respectable reputation in the community. If he had risen to officer status, he might well go on to a political career. The emperor made all the decisions, but the empire had an insatiable need for competent bureaucrats to carry them out.

Flavius Josephus, a Jew who fought against the Romans and lost, had nothing but admiration for the way they organized their army and trained their soldiers.

> Anyone who looks at the other parts of their military discipline will be forced to confess that they gained such a large dominion by their valor, and not just by luck. For they do not wait till war breaks out to begin to use their weapons ... but, as if their weapons always clung to them, they never have any rest from warlike exercises.

> And they do not wait till wartime to train their soldiers in using those weapons. Their military exercises are no different from the real use of their arms. Every soldier is exercised every day, and that with great diligence, as if a war were on already. That is why they bear the fatigue of battles so easily.[7]

He tells us something, too, about the combination of harsh discipline and lavish rewards that kept the soldiers motivated. It explains why Judah Ben-Hur's friend Messala was so keen on joining the Roman army: a man who started with nothing could go far if he worked at it.

> They manage the preparatory exercises of their weapons so that not just the bodies of the soldiers but also their souls may also become stronger. And they are moreover hardened for war by fear; for their laws inflict capital punishments, not only for soldiers who run away from their ranks, but for slothfulness and inactivity, even if it is only in a lesser degree. And their generals are more severe than their laws. But they prevent any suspicion of cruelty toward those under condemnation by the great rewards they bestow on the valiant soldiers.
>
> The readiness of obeying their commanders is so great that it is a fine sight to see in peace. But when they come to a battle, the whole army is but one body, so well coupled together are their ranks, so sudden are their turnings about, so sharp their hearing as to what orders are given them, so quick their sight of the standards, and

[7] Josephus, *Wars of the Jews*, bk. 3, chap. 5. All excerpts from *Wars of the Jews* are adapted from the translation by William Whiston.

> so nimble are their hands when they set to work. Thus whatever they do is done quickly, and what they suffer they bear with the greatest patience. Nor can we find any examples where they have been conquered in battle, when they came to a close fight, either by the multitude of the enemies, or by their stratagems, or by the difficulties in the places they were in; no, nor by fortune either, for their victories have been surer to them than fortune could have granted them. In a case, therefore, where counsel still goes before action, and where, after taking the best advice, that advice is followed by so active an army, what wonder is it that Euphrates on the east, the ocean on the west, the most fertile regions of Libya on the south, and the Danube and the Rhine on the north, are the limits of this empire? One might well say that the Roman possessions are not inferior to the Romans themselves.

After all this, Josephus seems to realize that he might have sounded a bit too effusive in his praise of his former enemies. He adds an explanation:

> I have given the reader this account, not so much with the intention of commending the Romans, as of comforting those who have been conquered by them, and to deter others from attempting revolutions under their government. This discourse of the Roman military conduct may also perhaps be of use to such of the curious as are ignorant of it, and yet have a mind to know it.

In other words: If, like me, you were defeated by the Romans, don't worry about it. It was inevitable. And if, like me, you're tempted to revolt against the Romans, just don't. Trust me.

In *Ben-Hur*, Judah's old friend Messala is supposed to have fought all over the Roman world, from snowy northern Europe to the deserts of Africa. That's actually typical of an ambitious Roman officer's career. Even the most ordinary soldier might see the empire from one end to the other in the course of his service.

This constant shuffling around had two interesting effects. One was that, as the Romans had probably calculated, it discouraged the soldiers from thinking in terms of regional loyalties. They saw the whole empire as a unit, and that was what they were devoted to—not to their own little corner of it. The other was that soldiers tended to spread new ideas very quickly from one end of the empire to the other, because there was always traffic going in all directions. A soldier who lived long enough to retire to a little farm somewhere had seen the world: he knew what people were thinking in Egypt and in Britain. That also tended to hold the empire together.

When an area was conquered, the Romans might do one of several things with it. They might leave the current ruler in charge, with the understanding that a certain amount of money would flow toward Rome every year, and with a Roman supervisor to make sure that the agreements were respected. This was a likely scenario if the local man in charge was Rome's ally: like the British centuries later, the Romans ended up with a lot of their possessions because some local warlord had begged them to come in and help him defeat some other local warlord. Thus Judea, for example, was ruled by King Herod when Jesus Christ was born. It was not because anyone thought Herod was a particularly competent ruler, but because he was Rome's ally, and that was his reward. Judea was a part of the Roman Empire in the sense that Rome ultimately controlled Judea's relations with the rest of the Roman world, but Herod was in charge of all the day-to-day ruling and could massacre children as much as he liked (see Matt. 2:16).

More usually, though, Rome would send a governor. In the late days of the Republic, these governors were a curse to the provinces they governed in Rome's name. Most of them saw their provinces as opportunities for plunder. The Senate in Rome might try to rein in their predatory behavior once in a while, but the Senate had enough troubles of its own, with constant civil wars and ambitious would-be dictators lopping off heads and displaying them in the Forum. It came to the point where the provincial governors ran their provinces practically as independent kingdoms, bilking as much as they could out of them. It took the strong hand of an emperor to make the governors responsible to Rome.

Even with all the shuffling around of soldiers and merchants, there was never a single language spoken across the whole Roman Empire. Instead, there were two. In the West, people spoke Latin, and in the East, they spoke Greek.

Alexander the Great had prepared the way in the East. His sprawling empire did not survive his death, but the smaller empires that succeeded it were founded by his Greek generals. After Alexander's conquests, Greek became the common language of the entire eastern Mediterranean.

There were also regional languages, of course: people in Judea, for example, still spoke Aramaic, a language common throughout the Middle East. But they would know enough Greek to get by in business: in fact, they were likely to be fluent in it. Look at the names of Jesus' disciples, and you see at once that many of them have both a Semitic name and a Greek name. Simon and Cephas, Thomas and Didymus, and, of course, Saul and Paul: a Jewish working-class man might have a Hebrew name for home and a Greek name for business with the Gentiles. (This is true in many Jewish neighborhoods in America today, where Hebrew names are used at home and American English names for business in the world at large.)

You could travel the entire eastern Mediterranean, from Egypt around through Judea and Syria, up into Asia Minor and across to Greece, and everywhere you went, you could make yourself understood in Greek.

The West spoke Latin. Again, there were some regional languages, but Latin was quickly displacing them except in the far frontiers. Even today, most of the former provinces of the empire in the West speak languages derived from Latin—Portuguese, Spanish, Catalan, French, Italian, with a pocket of Romanian in the East. That shows us how thoroughly Latinized the empire had become in the West. Even in Britain, where Latin never displaced the Celtic language of the inhabitants, the number of inscriptions in Latin shows us that you could get along in Latin, at least if you stuck to the cities.

So the empire was divided between a Latin-speaking West and a Greek-speaking East. But the division was not that simple, because people kept moving around. Remember that Pilate had the inscription on Jesus' cross written in three languages.

> Pilate also wrote a title and put it on the cross; it read, "Jesus of Nazareth, the King of the Jews." Many of the Jews read this title, for the place where Jesus was crucified was near the city; and it was written in Hebrew, in Latin, and in Greek. (John 19:19-20).

Hebrew probably means the closely related Aramaic, the everyday speech of people in first-century Palestine. There were enough Latin-speakers in Jerusalem — including Pilate himself and probably most of his soldiers — for a sign to be written in Latin as well as in Greek and Aramaic. If the hurriedly inscribed charge on Jesus' Cross was written that way, we can guess that there were probably many other trilingual signs in Jerusalem. In other words, the Roman Empire might have been something like Canada today, where a French-speaking inhabitant should be able to get by even in Manitoba, where hardly anyone speaks French as a native language.

It certainly worked the other way. Every educated person in the West studied Greek, because Greek was the language of culture. If you were a writer, you wrote in Greek if you wanted to be taken seriously as an intellectual. When Christians came to Rome, they had their liturgies in Greek for some time, and many of the earliest bishops of Rome — the first popes — have Greek names. When Paul wrote a letter to the Romans, he wrote it in Greek, not in Latin. Clearly he expected the church in Rome to understand his letter.

He had an attentive audience. Paul was bringing a new idea to Rome just at a time when Rome was desperately looking for something. Rome didn't know what it was looking for, but the old Roman religion just wasn't satisfying anymore.

What was the Roman religion? That is a question that would hardly make sense to a Roman. "Religion" in the abstract was a virtue, but what gods you worshipped was up to you. As long as you made your token submission to the idea of the empire by offering a little incense to the genius (a sort of pagan guardian angel) of the emperor, you could do pretty much what you liked. There was not a Roman religion: there was an almost infinite variety of cults, all operating on the "I'm okay, you're okay" principle.

The traditional religion of Rome was a mass of ancient legends and magical thinking, with a god or goddess for every occasion. Whatever you could think of, there was a god for that. Were the sewers backing up in the city? Perhaps there was trouble in the Cloaca Maxima, the Great Drain, which was one of the engineering marvels of the city of Rome. Well, there was a goddess for that: Cloacina, the goddess of the Cloaca Maxima.[8] Yes, you could actually pray to the goddess of the sewer. Whether she answered your prayers, and how she answered them, was up to her.

As the Roman world expanded, Romans came into contact with other religions of all sorts. Most of them were interpreted as local variations of Roman paganism. For example, the Romans aligned their own religion with the Greek mythology, making a more or less one-to-one correspondence between the gods of Greece and the gods of Rome. Zeus was Jupiter; Hera was Juno; Athena was Minerva; Hermes was Mercury; and so on. The occasional Greek god who had no obvious Roman equivalent—such as Apollo—was just absorbed into Roman thought with his Greek name intact. In the same way, the Romans conflated their own mythology with the much more ancient Egyptian pantheon and tended to see Egyptian gods and goddesses as equivalent to

[8] John G. Bourke: *Compilation of Notes and Memoranda Bearing upon the Use of Human Ordure and Human Urine in Rites of a Religious or Semi-Religious Character Among Various Nations* (Washington: War Department, 1888), 36.

their own. But, again, there were outliers. Like Apollo, Isis was adopted enthusiastically, and temples to Isis sprang up in Rome and all over the empire.

Apuleius's famous novel *Metamorphoses*, commonly called *The Golden Ass*, is a comic novel about a man who is transformed into a donkey, and all the hilarious misadventures he suffers. But behind the comedy, it's a tale of religious conversion: the man's life is not sorted out until he embraces the cult of Isis. In fact, the magical transformation into an ass represents what life is like before Isis steps in to sort it out. Apuleius was a clever writer who could have his comedy and his allegory too.

Mithras was another deity with a wide popularity in the empire. No one knows exactly what the cult of Mithras involved, because it was a *secret*, and even though there were Mithraeums in every city, the cult was good at keeping the secret. But it had something to do with Mithras, originally a Persian deity called Mithra, although the scanty evidence we have suggests that the cult went through a lot of changes from the Persian original as it filtered into the Roman Empire. He killed a bull, and in some way this had something to do with the salvation of his worshippers.

Salvation—there's a word that doesn't appear very often in Roman paganism. What many of these Eastern religions had in common was that they promised some sort of salvation or purification from sin. And that was something no one could get from traditional Roman religion, because traditional Roman religion didn't have much of an idea of sin.

Ordinary Roman paganism was very businesslike. You wanted something from the gods, so you bribed them with the appropriate offering, and they gave it to you. Or they didn't, either because they didn't like your bribe or just because they were capricious that way. It was good to do what was proper for the gods, in the same way that it was good to pay your bills or obey traffic laws. But Roman pagans didn't expect the gods to interfere with their inner lives very much. If you wanted to become a better person, you studied philosophy at one of the many schools set up by pedigreed Greek philosophers.

But just as Rome was reaching its peak of glory, Romans—especially educated Romans in the cities—were losing their faith in the old pagan gods. It might have seemed strange: clearly the Roman gods were winning. They led Rome's armies to conquer the world. Shouldn't every good Roman be grateful?

But, as we've already seen, the conquest of the world came with profound internal instability. A Roman who looked at the world empire of the late Republic might see nothing but corruption and decay. The provinces were being fleeced by petty tyrants who governed as they pleased. The famous Roman legions were being used almost entirely to fight other famous Roman legions. Blood flowed in the streets of Rome every day. Virtuous men were murdered by the latest transient dictator or took their own lives in despair. The world had gone wrong somehow. The Roman gods might have brought victory, but they couldn't fix what was broken.

And people began to wonder: Is it *I*? Is there something deeply wrong in my soul? Have I sinned?

This was a question the Roman gods couldn't answer. So the most thoughtful Romans started to look for other gods. They pulled them in from Egypt, from Persia, from Greece, from any cult that promised to fix what was broken inside themselves. Temples of strange foreign cults popped up like mushrooms all over the city of Rome, to the disgust of the few old-guard traditionalists who had not killed themselves.

Frequently these new cults proved just as businesslike as the old Roman pagan cults — indeed, sometimes even more nakedly businesslike. The historian Josephus tells us a story about how easily the priests of Isis were bribed.

There was a woman in Rome named Paulina, beautiful but unusually virtuous for the time. She was married to an equally virtuous husband, and she was a faithful devotee of Isis. A very rich aristocrat named Decius Mundus fell in love with her, but all his presents — even the offer of two hundred thousand drachmas — couldn't persuade her to spend one night with him.

Mundus, however, had a scheming freedwoman as his servant, and this woman told him she had a cunning plan that would cost him only fifty thousand drachmas. She went to the priests of Isis and bribed them with the fifty thousand drachmas to tell Paulina that she had been summoned to spend the night with the god Anubis, who had fallen in love with her. Paulina, faithful to the cult, told her husband that she was going to the temple to spend the night with Anubis, and he said, "Sure, go ahead" — either believing that this was some metaphorical religious ceremony or sharing his wife's simple faith: Josephus doesn't tell us anything other than that he trusted her chastity completely.

So she went and spent the night at the temple, and you can guess who played the part of Anubis.

Paulina was very proud of herself. A god had come to lie with her! She told her husband. She told all her friends.

It wasn't until three days later that Mundus saw her in the street and simply couldn't resist bragging. "Well, Paulina," he said, "you have saved me two hundred thousand drachmas, a sum you might have added to your own family. Yet you have not failed to be at my service just the way I wanted. As for the insults you heaped on Mundus, I care nothing for names; but I rejoice in the pleasure I gained by what I did while I took to myself the name of ..."—we imagine a big leer at this point—"Anubis."

The deception did not go unpunished. Deeply ashamed but still true to her husband, Paulina revealed everything to him. And her husband went straight to the emperor Tiberius. Josephus tells us that Tiberius "examined" the priests of Isis, and we can be sure that this "examination" involved some enhanced interrogation techniques. The priests who perpetrated the deception and the servant woman who had invented the scheme were all crucified. The temple of Isis was demolished, and the statue of Isis thrown into the Tiber. But the cult didn't stay out of Rome long.

As for Mundus, the actual rapist, Tiberius only banished him from Rome, "because he supposed that what crime he had committed was done out of the passion of love."[9] Boys will be boys, after all.

This tragic little farce, or farcical tragedy, gives us a glimpse of culture among the upper classes, the intellectual and moral leaders of ancient Rome. A virtuous wife is a strange anomaly. An aristocrat who "falls in love" with her—meaning that he wants to spend one night with her and then doesn't care if she kills herself—can practice almost any deception and have the sympathy of the other aristocrats. Priests of pagan cults are corrupt, selling their religion for what Mundus considered a bargain-basement price—remember that he was willing to pay Paulina herself four times as much for a single night.

[9] Josephus, *Antiquities of the Jews*, bk. 18, chap. 3. All excerpts from *Antiquities of the Jews* are adapted from the translation by William Whiston.

And finally, the ancient pagan religion is not satisfying anymore. Even the highest classes of people are looking elsewhere for what the Roman gods can't give them. In the midst of peace and prosperity throughout the world, Romans have a strong sense that they themselves are morally broken. They look to foreign cults that promise not material success, but deliverance from sin.

In fact, Romans searched so far and wide for new religious ideas that some even found them among the Jews.

4

Roman Judea: Ben-Hur's Political World

One province gave the Roman Empire more trouble than any of the others. It was a province filled with religious fanatics so stubborn that they refused to offer a pinch of incense at the altar of the emperor's genius and so fanatical that any perceived insult to their religion could send them into a bloody rebellion that would take the might of several legions to put down.

That province was Judea, the land of the Jews—and of course we have described it from the point of view of the Romans. From the point of view of many Judeans, the Romans were another in a long line of hostile occupying powers bent on forcing the nation of Israel to give up its loyalty to the one true God.

The central city of Judea was Jerusalem, the ancient City of David. Let us begin our visit to Judea with a trip to the market in Jerusalem, as it was imagined by Lew Wallace—who, as you will remember, had spent years in making sure that he had research to back up every detail of the scene.

> Here stands a donkey, dozing under panniers full of lentils, beans, onions, and cucumbers, brought fresh from the gardens and terraces of Galilee. When not engaged

in serving customers, the master, in a voice which only the initiated can understand, cries his stock. Nothing can be simpler than his costume—sandals, and an unbleached, undyed blanket, crossed over one shoulder and girt round the waist. Near-by, and far more imposing and grotesque, though scarcely as patient as the donkey, kneels a camel, raw-boned, rough, and gray, with long shaggy tufts of fox-colored hair under its throat, neck, and body, and a load of boxes and baskets curiously arranged upon an enormous saddle. The owner is an Egyptian, small, lithe, and of a complexion which has borrowed a good deal from the dust of the roads and the sands of the desert. He wears a faded tarbooshe, a loose gown, sleeveless, unbelted, and dropping from the neck to the knee. His feet are bare. The camel, restless under the load, groans and occasionally shows his teeth; but the man paces indifferently to and fro, holding the driving-strap, and all the time advertising his fruits fresh from the orchards of the Kedron—grapes, dates, figs, apples, and pomegranates.

At the corner where the lane opens out into the court, some women sit with their backs against the gray stones of the wall. Their dress is that common to the humbler classes of the country—a linen frock extending the full length of the person, loosely gathered at the waist, and a veil or wimple broad enough, after covering the head, to wrap the shoulders. Their merchandise is contained in a number of earthen jars, such as are still used in the East for bringing water from the wells, and some leathern bottles. Among the jars and bottles, rolling upon the stony floor, regardless of the crowd and cold, often in danger but never hurt, play half a dozen half-naked children, their brown bodies, jetty eyes, and thick black hair attesting the blood of Israel. Sometimes, from under the wimples, the mothers look up, and in the vernacular modestly bespeak their trade: in the bottles "honey of grapes," in the jars "strong drink." Their entreaties are usually lost in the general uproar, and they fare illy against the many competitors: brawny fellows with bare legs, dirty tunics, and long beards, going about with bottles lashed to their backs, and shouting "Honey of wine! Grapes of En-Gedi!" When a customer halts one of them, round comes the bottle, and, upon lifting the thumb from the nozzle, out into the ready cup gushes the deep-red blood of the luscious berry.

Scarcely less blatant are the dealers in birds—doves, ducks, and frequently the singing bulbul, or nightingale, most frequently pigeons; and buyers, receiving them from the nets, seldom fail to think of the perilous life of the catchers, bold climbers of the cliffs; now hanging with hand and foot to the face of the crag, now swinging in a basket far down the mountain fissure.

Blent with peddlers of jewelry—sharp men cloaked in scarlet and blue, top-heavy under prodigious white turbans, and fully conscious of the power there is in the lustre of a ribbon and the incisive gleam of gold, whether in bracelet or necklace, or in rings for the finger or the nose—and with peddlers of household utensils, and with dealers in wearing-apparel, and with retailers of unguents for anointing the person, and with hucksters of all articles, fanciful as well as of need, hither and thither, tugging at halters and ropes, now screaming, now coaxing, toil

> the venders of animals—donkeys, horses, calves, sheep, bleating kids, and awkward camels; animals of every kind except the outlawed swine.[10]

The exotic sights, sounds, and smells would have instantly reminded a Roman soldier that he wasn't in Rome anymore. Yet there were cities in the Middle East where a Roman would feel very much at home. Caesarea Maritima, a port city near modern Tel Aviv, was planned by the Romans and named after Caesar Augustus, and it looked pretty much like every Roman city in the provinces.

Those two cities—Caesarea and Jerusalem—stood almost as visual metaphors for the state of the Roman province of Judea.

Caesarea was the Roman administrative capital. It was flat, with straight streets in a grid pattern. You always knew where you were and how to find your way to any other part of the city. The architecture was interchangeable with the architecture of any other city the Romans had founded in their vast possessions. In the same way that a suburban American can find the same chain restaurants and big-box stores in Maine and Arizona, Alaska and Florida, a Roman from anywhere else in the empire could feel comfortably at home in Caesarea. It was the old cities, such as Jerusalem, where a Roman might feel out of place.

Jerusalem was immemorially ancient, built on precipitous hills, with streets that wandered in all directions. It was easy to get lost in narrow dark alleys. And if you were a Roman, you must have had the vague sense of being surrounded by people who wanted to kill you.

[10] *Ben-Hur*, bk. 1, chap. 6.

Ben-Hur's Political World

For Rome, the Middle East was a land of perpetual trouble. It was filled with religious extremists who could turn into terrorists whenever their delicate religious sensibilities were offended by some perfectly ordinary operation of the imperial government. And it wasn't just that the inhabitants wanted to kill the Romans. They were always trying to kill each other, too.

To understand how Jewish politics got to be such a mess, we need to understand a little of Jewish history.

Your Bible will tell you most of the history of Israel from the Exodus from Egypt on up to the victory of the Maccabees. (At least if it's a Catholic Bible. Protestant Bibles leave out the books of Maccabees, or put them in a separate section of Apocrypha, which are books Protestants consider good to read but not canonical Scripture.) Let's take it at a gallop.

Abraham was promised by God that the land of Canaan would belong to him and his descendants forever. But in the time of his grandson Jacob, who was also known as Israel, there was a terrible famine in the land. Egypt, however, had plenty of food, thanks to the foresight of Jacob's son Joseph, who had been sold by his jealous brothers as a slave and had risen to be prime minister in Egypt. Jacob and the whole family moved to Egypt, and the Israelites prospered there until a new Egyptian pharaoh "who did not know Joseph" (Exod. 1:8) enslaved them all. This Egyptian slavery was remembered ever after as the prototypical bondage from which God delivered his people in the Exodus.

Moses led the Exodus from Egypt. But because of their faithlessness, the Israelites spent forty years in the wilderness on their way back to the Promised Land of Canaan. In the wilderness they received the Law at Mount Sinai, which gave them the customs that made Israel a distinct people among the nations.

Israel conquered Canaan, the Promised Land, but was constantly seduced by the cults of the Canaanites' gods. As the Bible historians tell it, every lapse from pure faith in God led to troubles from strong enemies, which would be overcome only when the people remembered who they were and prayed to God to send a deliverer.

After a long period of near anarchy punctuated by occasional deliverers—the Judges—the tribes of Israel demanded a king. King Saul didn't work out—he had faithlessness issues again. King David built the tribes of Israel into a powerful kingdom, and his son Solomon made the kingdom a small empire. But Solomon was seduced by the foreign gods of his many wives, and after Solomon, the empire split in two. The old story was repeated: according to the Bible historians, lapses into idolatry brought invasions from powerful empires. The prophets warned the people to turn back to their God, but the people wouldn't listen. Eventually both halves—Israel in the north and Judah in the south—were conquered. Israel was dispersed, but the upper classes of Judah returned after decades in exile in Babylon and rebuilt Jerusalem.

This Babylonian exile and subsequent return was another of the formative experiences of Israel: from it the prophets learned that God would redeem his people even from the worst circumstances, if only they would repent and turn back to their true faith. As a practical matter of history, it established large populations of Jews in various places: most notably in Babylon, but also in Egypt, and soon wherever trade and commerce took them.

The remnant of Israel prospered under Persian domination, but after Alexander, it came under various Greek empires.

When one of the Greek rulers attempted to paganize Jerusalem, it touched off a rebellion—with the Maccabees as heroes of the story—that ended in independence for Judea.

That's as far as our Bible takes us. And we can see that the story the Bible historians tell always has the same moral. God's people are punished for abandoning the Law they received at Sinai, but if they return to God and the Law, God will rescue them. This is the story that any Judean child would have learned at his mother's knee. It's the story that every Judean citizen knew by heart.

And there was one more thing they knew. They believed—or most of them did—that God had at least one more trick up his sleeve. Someday, when things looked bleak, God would send a Son of David to rescue them and establish his kingdom permanently. The Lord's Anointed—"Messiah" in Hebrew, "Christ" in Greek—would liberate his people from their oppressors. It might happen any day now.

❧

So what happened after the story in our Old Testament? There's a long gap between the Maccabees and the New Testament, but we have plenty of other historical sources to fill it in.The victory of the Maccabees did not mean that everybody lived happily ever after. That never happens in history. Instead, various greedy and corrupt rulers fought each other for the throne, as usual.

Meanwhile, two major parties grew up in Jewish politics. Since there weren't elections, the parties didn't operate the way political parties do today: instead, they were networks made up of religious beliefs and personal loyalties.

The Sadducees were generally the party of the priests. They probably thought of themselves as the enlightened thinkers of the day, which is to say that they didn't really believe in a lot of the religious nonsense that the common people believed in. For example, they denied the resurrection. Luke tells us how they provoked a debate with Jesus by asking him what they probably thought was an unanswerable question:

> There came to him some Sadducees, those who say that there is no resurrection, and they asked him a question, saying, "Teacher, Moses wrote for us that if a man's brother dies, having a wife but no children, the man must take the wife and raise up children for his brother. Now there were seven brothers; the first took a wife, and died without children; and the second and the third took her, and likewise all seven left no children and died. Afterward the woman also died. In the resurrection, therefore, whose wife will the woman be? For the seven had her as wife."
>
> And Jesus said to them, "The sons of this age marry and are given in marriage; but those who are accounted worthy to attain to that age and to the resurrection from the dead neither marry nor are given in marriage, for they cannot die any more, because they are equal to angels and are sons of God, being sons of the resurrection. But that the dead are raised, even Moses showed, in the passage about the bush, where he calls the Lord the God of Abraham and the God of Isaac and the God of Jacob. Now he is not God of the dead, but of the living; for all live to him."
>
> And some of the scribes answered, "Teacher, you have spoken well." For they no longer dared to ask him any question. (Luke 20:27-40)

Sadducees were also much more open to influence from outside. They could easily pick up the ways of the Greeks and Romans around them—not worshipping their gods, of course, but picking up their fashions and ideas.

The other party was the Pharisees. They went to exactly the opposite extreme: they emphasized and exaggerated the differences between themselves and the non-Jews around them. Jesus said that "they make their phylacteries broad and their fringes long" (Matt. 23:5), pointing out two distinctive aspects of Jewish dress that the Pharisees carried to showy excess.

The Pharisees believed that the only way to be faithful to God was to separate themselves entirely from the Gentiles—the people around them who were not Jewish. They elaborated the Law of Moses into a strict code of behavior and fashion that got harder and harder to follow as the elaborations multiplied.

Of course, they were not all simply hypocrites or fanatics. There was good reason for their belief: at every turn the Israelite nation had been betrayed by people who compromised with outsiders. Certainly many of the Pharisees were moved by a sincere belief that God's Law was the only true law and a sincere desire to follow the Law to the letter.

Josephus explains the differences between the two sects, and adds one other big difference: the difference of class.

> What I want to explain now is this: the Pharisees have delivered to the people a great many observances by succession from their fathers, which are not written in the law of Moses. That is why the Sadducees reject them: they say that we are to treat those observances that are in the written word as obligatory, but are not to observe ones that are derived from the tradition of our forefathers.

> These are the things that produce the great disputes and differences that have arisen among them. But the Sadducees are able to persuade none but the rich; the people do not respect them. The Pharisees, however, have the multitude on their side.[11]

So those were the two political parties—the Democrats and Republicans, the Labor and Tory Parties of Judea. As you can guess, they hated each other.

The Pharisees thought the Sadducees were sellouts—people who had betrayed Israel in return for the comforts of Greek and Roman style and the money that came to friends of the great imperial powers. The Sadducees thought the Pharisees were a bunch of hypocritical fanatics who wanted to take Israel back to the dark ages. The two groups had bitter fights—sometimes riots, sometimes civil wars. And, as always happens, after a while the fight was more about the fight than about any of the principles it had started with.

During one of those periodic fights between Pharisees and Sadducees, the Romans wandered in and took over. It was a typical Roman conquest. The Romans didn't even set out to conquer Judea. But there were two brothers fighting for the throne—one sympathetic to the Sadducees, one to the Pharisees. The Romans had just conquered Syria, with Judea as the ally of Rome. Both brothers sent bribes to the Roman general begging for his support; the Roman simply had to sit back and look as if he were thinking hard, and the bribes got bigger and bigger. In effect, the Romans were auctioning Roman domination to the highest bidder.

[11] Josephus, *Antiquities*, bk. 13, chap. 10.

Eventually the Roman general Pompey the Great chose the brother named Hyrcanus, figuring he was the weaker of the two and therefore the one who could be more easily managed. His brother Aristobulus surrendered without a serious fight and promised to open up Jerusalem to the Romans. The people of Jerusalem resisted for a while, but Pompey was too much for them. Hyrcanus was king of Judea, but with a Roman governor to help supervise trade and make sure the proper amount of money was flowing back to Rome.

Hyrcanus had an adviser named Antipater—a scheming minister straight out of Central Casting. Antipater managed to find plum positions for all his cronies, and in particular for his son Herod. That name probably sounds familiar to you, because after a certain number of murders and civil wars, Herod managed to make himself king of Judea.

Herod was still under the thumb of the Romans, of course. But as long as the money kept coming in to Rome, the Romans didn't much care how awful Herod was.

And Herod was truly awful. Many Gospel readers probably think, or hope, that the massacre of the innocents, Herod's murder of all the boys under two years old in Bethlehem, is a legend. But it was perfectly in character for Herod.

Herod was an Idumean, from an area south of Judea whose residents had been forced to convert to Judaism by an earlier Judean conquest. Herod always portrayed himself as a faithful Jew, but he lived a life of appalling decadence. He had ten wives at various times and numerous children. He executed one of his wives, Mariamne I (he had two wives named Mariamne), for treason. He had his sons Aristobulus and Alexander executed for treason as well. Josephus describes how he acted at their trial:

> Herod came by himself alone, and accused his sons—and he did it as if it were not a melancholy accusation that he would not have made if it were not absolutely necessary, considering his difficulties. No, he did it in such a way as was very indecent for a father to accuse his sons, for he was very enthusiastic and unbalanced when he came to the demonstration of the crime they were accused of, and gave the greatest signs of passion and barbarity. He would not allow the judges to consider of the weight of the evidence, but asserted the accusations to be true by his own authority, after a manner most indecent in a father against his sons.[12]

The sons were not allowed to speak in their own defense, and the judges were forced to render a guilty verdict. When supporters of his sons begged Herod to reconsider, he had three hundred of them executed for treason, too. About three years after that, Herod had his son Antipater II executed for treason—an execution that required the approval of the Roman emperor Augustus. Yet through all this, Herod kept up a show of being faithful to Jewish law. He might murder his own family, but he never touched pork.

Augustus was privileged to see Herod from a distance and could afford to be amused by the irony. "Better to be Herod's pig than Herod's son,"[13] he said, neatly summing up Herod's whole personality in a few words.

[12] Josephus, *Antiquities*, bk. 16, chap. 11.

[13] "Melius est Herodis porcum esse quam filium." Macrobius, *Saturnalia* 2:4. New translation from the Latin text at http://penelope.uchicago.edu/Thayer/L/Roman/Texts/Macrobius/Saturnalia/2*.html.

When Herod lay dying in Jericho—in a horrible and painful way—he summoned all the most important men in Judea. He had them all placed under guard in the hippodrome (the racetrack) and then revealed one last utterly mad scheme to his sister Salome and her husband, Alexas. "He was not unacquainted with the temper of the Jews," Josephus says, "that his death would be a thing very desirable, and exceedingly acceptable to them." But he would make sure there was no rejoicing.

> He would have a great mourning at his funeral, and such as never any king had before him; for the whole nation would mourn from their very soul, which otherwise would be done in sport and mockery only. As soon as they saw he had given up the ghost, they should place soldiers around the hippodrome, while they do not know that he is dead; and they should not declare his death to the multitude until they had given orders to have those who were in custody shot with arrows.... [Thus] he should have the honor of a memorable mourning at his funeral.[14]

Yes, that would have been memorable, wouldn't it? The next time you're tempted to think that the massacre of the innocents at Bethlehem was a fable, remember that Herod intended to make sure there was enough weeping at his own funeral by killing all the prominent men in his dominion. Fortunately, his sister didn't do it. As soon as Herod died, she turned the men loose: "But then Salome and Alexas, before the king's death was made known, dismissed those that were shut up in the hippodrome, and told them that the king ordered them to go away to their

[14] Josephus, *Antiquities*, bk. 17, chap. 6.

own lands, and take care of their own affairs, which was esteemed by the nation a great benefit." You can bet it was.

Long after he was dead, Herod's shadow loomed large over Judea. He was a builder on a colossal scale: he had built the quintessentially Roman city of Caesarea Maritima and rebuilt the Temple in Jerusalem to be one of the architectural marvels of the world. And his family still infested the government in various capacities.

After Herod, the Romans decided that Judea would be better off as a province rather than a nominal kingdom. Three of Herod's surviving sons became tetrarchs (the word actually means ruler of a quarter, but obviously it was used loosely), but no one was king, and Rome ruled the province more directly.

Surprisingly enough, things got even worse.

Romans had a hard time understanding the Jewish religion, but they knew it meant constant trouble from radical elements. Jews were extremely stubborn about offering anything on pagan altars, and the Romans found that the only way to get along with their Judean subjects was to exempt them from the requirement of making token offerings to the Roman gods. The Romans didn't really understand the objection, but they did understand that the Jews had an ancient tradition that went back thousands of years. They respected that. Ancient traditions had proved their worth by lasting long enough to be ancient.

Still, there was something contemptible about Jewish religion to many educated Romans. In the common movement of people hither and yon, Jews were everywhere in the empire. And everywhere they went, they kept their distinct dress and customs. Externally it was hard to tell a devotee of one pagan god from a devotee of another; but you always knew who was a Jew. When a Roman governor came to Judea, it was usually hard for him to disguise his contempt for the superstitious nonsense he had to put up with from the locals.

Lew Wallace had his Messala express an epitome of the Roman attitude toward all things Jewish:

> "By the drunken son of Semele, what it is to be a Jew! All men and things, even heaven and earth, change; but a Jew never. To him there is no backward, no forward; he is what his ancestor was in the beginning. In this sand I draw you a circle—there! Now tell me what more a Jew's life is? Round and round, Abraham here, Isaac and Jacob yonder, God in the middle. And the circle—by the master of all thunders! the circle is too large. I draw it again—" He stopped, put his thumb upon the ground, and swept the fingers about it. "See, the thumb spot is the Temple, the finger-lines Judea. Outside the little space is there nothing of value? The arts! Herod was a builder; therefore he is accursed. Painting, sculpture! to look upon them is sin. Poetry you make fast to your altars. Except in the synagogue, who of you attempts eloquence? In war all you conquer in the six days you lose on the seventh. Such your life and limit; who shall say no if I laugh at you? Satisfied with the worship of such a people, what is your God to our Roman Jove, who lends us his eagles that we may compass the universe with our arms? Hillel, Simeon, Shammai, Abtalion—what are they to the masters who teach that everything is worth knowing that can be known?"[15]

[15] *Ben-Hur*, bk. 2, chap. 2.

To a Roman, Jews were superstitious fanatics who refused to come to grips with the modern world. And lazy! Why, they stopped work one day out of every seven. Can you imagine that? (Of course, the Romans had about as many holidays scattered throughout the year as the Jews had sabbaths, but that was *different*.)

Even so, there were some among the Romans who looked at the Jewish way of life and admired what they saw. And there were some among the Jews who were very welcoming to these Gentiles. There were converts who even underwent circumcision as adults in order to become fully and properly Jews. But there was also a large group of "God-fearers"—Gentiles who listened to the teachings at the synagogue and believed that the God of the Jews was the one true God. There were schools set up in Rome to teach Gentiles the Jewish philosophy. We know that because Josephus tells us about one that was run by a crook:

> There was a man who was a Jew, but had been driven away from his own country by an accusation laid against him for violating their laws, and by the fear he was under of punishment for that violation. He was in all respects a wicked man. Living in Rome, he professed to instruct men in the wisdom of the laws of Moses. He procured also three other men, entirely of the same character with himself, to be his partners. These men persuaded Fulvia, a woman of great dignity, and one that had embraced the Jewish religion, to send purple and gold to the temple at Jerusalem; and, when they had gotten them, they employed them for their own uses, and spent the money themselves—which was why they had asked her for it in the first place.

Once again the matter was reported to the emperor Tiberius himself, and he reacted even more extremely than he had in the case of Paulina, the devotee of Isis: he banished every last one of the Jews from Rome. There were thousands of them at the time: four thousand Jewish men were sent to Sardinia, but "a greater number," says Josephus, were punished for refusing to serve as soldiers "on account of keeping the laws of their forefathers."[16]

From this story we learn that certain Romans of the upper classes were turning to the Jewish religion for the spiritual certainty they couldn't find elsewhere. This Fulvia is obviously a woman with money, and "of great dignity" implies that she belongs to the highest classes.

Josephus is not the only writer who tells us about these God fearers. You may remember one of the stories in the Acts of the Apostles:

> At Caesarea there was a man named Cornelius, a centurion of what was known as the Italian Cohort, a devout man who feared God with all his household, gave alms liberally to the people, and prayed constantly to God. (Acts 10:1-2)

Cornelius is a good Latin name, and he is an important officer in the "Italian cohort"—a Roman soldier far away from home in the Middle East. And he prays every day to the Jewish God and tries to live his life according to the most important precepts of the Jewish Law, especially the parts about giving alms to the poor.

In the story, Cornelius has a vision of an angel telling him to send for Peter. Meanwhile, Peter has a vision telling him that all foods are clean for Christ's followers. Thus, Cornelius and his whole family are baptized. When we read this story, we usually get the most important point of it, which is that Gentiles won't

[16] Josephus, *Antiquities*, bk. 18, chap. 3.

be held to the Jewish dietary laws. But we often miss the interesting background that Cornelius was already a "God fearer"—a man who already worshipped the one God whom the Jews believed in, even though he was a Roman officer from Italy.

Most of the Romans sent to occupy Judea were not so sympathetic. One in particular stands out as an epitome of the clash between Roman and Jewish culture: Pontius Pilate, whom we remember as the man who allowed Jesus of Nazareth to be crucified.

Pilate was always in hot water. He never knew quite what to do with the Judean populace and their strange prejudices. Sometimes he tried to be conciliatory; sometimes he tried to be stern. And whatever he did, it was usually the wrong choice.

Our friend Josephus gives us a good example of Pilate's stubbornness.

> But now Pilate, the procurator of Judea, moved the army from Cesarea to Jerusalem, to take their winter quarters there, in order to abolish the Jewish laws.
>
> So he introduced Caesar's effigies, which were on the standards, and brought them into the city. But our law forbids us the very making of images, for which reason the former procurators used to make their entry into the city with standards that did not have those ornaments. Pilate was the first who brought those images to Jerusalem, and set them up there; which was done without the knowledge of the people, because it was done in the night-time.
>
> But as soon as they knew it, they came in multitudes to Caesarea, and interceded with Pilate many days, that

> he would remove the images. He would not grant their requests, because it would tend to the injury of Caesar. Yet they persevered in their request.
>
> On the sixth day he ordered his soldiers to have their weapons privately, while he came and sat upon his judgment-seat, which seat was so prepared in the open place of the city, that it concealed the army that lay ready to oppress them; and when the Jews petitioned him again, he gave a signal to the soldiers to surround them, and threatened that their punishment should be no less than immediate death, unless they would leave off disturbing him, and go their ways home.
>
> But they threw themselves upon the ground, and laid their necks bare, and said they would take their death very willingly, rather than the wisdom of their laws should be transgressed. Pilate was deeply affected with their firm resolution to keep their laws inviolable, and presently commanded the images to be carried back from Jerusalem to Caesarea.[17]

It's nice that Pilate decided not to kill all the protesters. But he came close. What did his Jewish subjects learn from the experience? It looks as though they were learning that they could manipulate Pilate is they put up enough of a fuss.

It didn't always work, though. Sometimes Pilate decided he had just had enough of these stubborn fanatics. Josephus tells us how Pilate built an aqueduct to bring in fresh water for Jerusalem. What could be more unobjectionable than that? Unfortunately, he used the Temple funds, which caused a riot.

[17] Ibid.

> But Pilate undertook to bring a current of water to Jerusalem, and did it with the sacred money, and derived the origin of the stream from the distance of two hundred furlongs. However, the Jews were not pleased with what had been done about this water; and many ten thousands of the people got together, and made a clamor against him, and insisted that he should leave off that design. Some of them also used reproaches, and abused the man, as crowds of such people usually do. So he habited a great number of his soldiers in their habit, who carried daggers under their garments, and sent them to a place where they might surround them. So he bade the Jews himself go away; but they boldly casting reproaches upon him, he gave the soldiers that signal which had been beforehand agreed on; who laid upon them much greater blows than Pilate had commanded then, and equally punished those that were tumultuous, and those that were not, nor did they spare them in the least; and since the people were unarmed, and were caught by men prepared for what they were about, there were a great number of them slain by this means, and others of them ran away wounded; and thus an end was put to this sedition.[18]

When *Ben-Hur* portrays the Roman soldiers as thugs, alternately suspicious and contemptuous of the locals, and ready to kill anyone who gets in their way—well, it's just being true to history. That was what Judea was like: the ordinary citizens were caught between fanatical terrorists and a brutal occupying army.

This was the world Jesus and his disciples knew.

[18] Ibid.

5

Jesus: The Man and the Movement

Imagine yourself in that colorful market that Lew Wallace described so thoroughly. You wander through the market in Jerusalem, looking for nothing in particular. You've already done the shopping for the day, and you have all the pomegranates you need. But it's such a colorful place that you can't help just ambling up and down past the stalls to see what might be on offer. Colorful fabrics flap in the breeze; pottery of all descriptions is piled up at the potter's stall; and over here is a fine selection of useful things made of wood.

You stop for a moment. The craftsman has skill: you can see that at once. His meticulous work is done with love and attention. And when he greets you, there's something about that voice—even with its obvious Galilean accent. What is it about that voice? Why does it make you want to stop and listen to this simple carpenter all day?

❧

The novel *Ben-Hur* covers a longer span of time than the movie. In Lew Wallace's story, Judah Ben-Hur and Jesus of Nazareth are about the same age. They first meet as Judah—a teenager in the book—is being taken away from his home to be sentenced to the galleys. The Romans have been dragging an utterly exhausted Judah behind them over the dusty road when they come across Joseph of Nazareth, a carpenter whom Wallace takes the liberty of imagining as a rabbi as well. Curious bystanders persuade the venerable Joseph to ask the Roman officer in charge about the prisoner. The answer is that this is the son of the noble Prince Hur and that he is accused of attempting to assassinate the Roman procurator.

"Did he kill him?" asked the rabbi.

"No."

"He is under sentence."

"Yes—the galleys for life."

"The Lord help him!" said Joseph, for once moved out of his stolidity.

Thereupon a youth who came up with Joseph, but had stood behind him unobserved, laid down an axe he had been carrying, and, going to the great stone standing by the well, took from it a pitcher of water. The action was so quiet that before the guard could interfere, had they been disposed to do so, he was stooping over the prisoner, and offering him drink.

The hand laid kindly upon his shoulder awoke the unfortunate Judah, and, looking up, he saw a face he never forgot—the face of a boy about his own age, shaded by locks of yellowish bright chestnut hair; a face lighted by dark-blue eyes, at the time so soft, so appealing, so full of love and holy purpose, that they had all the power of command and will. The spirit of the Jew, hardened though it was by days and nights of suffering, and so embittered by wrong that its dreams of revenge took

> in all the world, melted under the stranger's look, and became as a child's. He put his lips to the pitcher, and drank long and deep. Not a word was said to him, nor did he say a word.
>
> When the draught was finished, the hand that had been resting upon the sufferer's shoulder was placed upon his head, and stayed there in the dusty locks time enough to say a blessing; the stranger then returned the pitcher to its place on the stone, and, taking his axe again, went back to Rabbi Joseph. All eyes went with him, the decurion's as well as those of the villagers.
>
> This was the end of the scene at the well. When the men had drunk, and the horses, the march was resumed. But the temper of the decurion was not as it had been; he himself raised the prisoner from the dust, and helped him on a horse behind a soldier. The Nazarenes went to their houses—among them Rabbi Joseph and his apprentice.
>
> And so, for the first time, Judah and the son of Mary met and parted.[19]

You'll notice that the "son of Mary" doesn't say anything. When Wallace made up his mind to write a novel with Jesus Christ as one of the characters, he knew that he was treading on thin ice—all the more so because, at the time, he wasn't a Christian himself. Any accusations of irreverence would doom his novel: no one would read it. So he made up his mind not to write any dialogue for Jesus that was not actually recorded in the Gospels. This scene, in which our teenage hero meets the teenage Jesus, is the only incident Wallace added to Jesus' life

[19] *Ben-Hur*, bk. 2, chap. 7.

completely from his own imagination. Most readers will probably agree that it's believable: it's the sort of thing we think Jesus *would* have done as a teenager.

One of the big attractions of *Ben-Hur* is that it gives us a chance to see Jesus Christ the way other people might have seen him in his own time. In our imagination, we strip away the centuries of accumulated tradition and look at Jesus with fresh eyes. Who was this carpenter from Nazareth? Just describing him that way makes him sound so insignificant: "Can anything good come out of Nazareth?" as Nathanael asked (John 1:46), probably repeating the punch line of a popular joke. How could an ordinary craftsman from the backwoods hill country change the whole world so completely?

In *Ben-Hur*, we share the baffling, exciting, confusing, upsetting, and life-changing experience of discovering Jesus of Nazareth for the first time. We may be surprised to find him looking so *ordinary*. But that's what the Gospels tell us: people who had known Jesus all his life thought of him as just an ordinary workman. When he went back to Nazareth, he could hardly find anyone to listen to him.

> And on the sabbath he began to teach in the synagogue; and many who heard him were astonished, saying, "Where did this man get all this? What is the wisdom given to him? What mighty works are wrought by his hands! Is not this the carpenter, the son of Mary and brother of James and Joses and Judas and Simon, and are not his sisters here with us?" And they took offense at him.
>
> And Jesus said to them, "A prophet is not without honor, except in his own country, and among his own kin, and in his own house." (Mark 6:2-4)

The people around Nazareth had a hard time thinking about Jesus as a teacher or a prophet. They knew him too well. They knew his mother and his cousins. His whole extended family was a familiar sight. To the people of his hometown, Jesus was always a carpenter, the son of a carpenter, a man who worked with saws and planes.

We have some of the same problem, except in reverse. We've always known Jesus as the Christ, the Son of God. We can't see him as an ordinary craftsman who made things with his hands and sold them to customers. Yes, we know *intellectually* that he did that—otherwise the Nazareth passage in Matthew and Mark doesn't make sense. But we can't *imagine* him doing it.

Ben-Hur helps us imagine Jesus the man, the strangely ordinary carpenter who did and said such extraordinary things.

Whenever a prophet who spoke with great confidence and wisdom came around, the people of Judea always began to ask themselves the same thing: Is this the Messiah? Is this the Christ? Is this the Anointed One of God?

When John the Baptist started preaching in the wilderness and attracting big crowds, the question naturally came up.

> And this is the testimony of John, when the Jews sent priests and Levites from Jerusalem to ask him, "Who are you?" He confessed, he did not deny, but confessed, "I am not the Christ." (John 1:19-20)

They believed that the Messiah would liberate them from the power of the Romans and establish the kingdom of Israel as a great power. Naturally, the Romans were always just a little worried about potential messiahs. So were the Sadducees, the upper classes who had much to lose and nothing to gain from a break with Rome.

That explains some of Jesus' behavior in the earlier part of his ministry.

> "Who do men say that I am?"
>
> And they told him, "John the Baptist; and others say, Elijah; and others one of the prophets."
>
> And he asked them, "But who do you say that I am?"
>
> Peter answered him, "You are the Christ."
>
> And he charged them to tell no one about him. (Mark 8:27-30)

That last line—repeated many times in the Gospel of Mark—always baffles us. Isn't the whole point that everyone should know the Messiah has come? But Jesus knew what he was doing. If people thought he was claiming to be the Messiah at the beginning of his ministry, there would never be a rest of his ministry.

Throughout the relatively short time he spent preaching in Galilee and Judea, Jesus refused to meet people's expectations of what the Messiah would do. The rich and the ostentatiously virtuous sneered, "This man receives sinners and eats with them!" (Luke 15:2). It was the poor and lowly who seriously asked, "Can this be the Christ?" (John 4:29).

The movie *Ben-Hur* gives us a good picture of those reactions. Judah, from a rich family, is dubious about the carpenter with all his strange talk about loving one's enemies. It's the poor who are enthralled by him. Only when Judah has lost everything does he have a chance to see Jesus of Nazareth for who he really is.

Even Jesus' closest disciples didn't understand the nature of his kingdom.

> Then the mother of the sons of Zebedee came up to him, with her sons, and kneeling before him she asked him for something.
>
> And he said to her, "What do you want?"
>
> She said to him, "Command that these two sons of mine may sit, one at your right hand and one at your left, in your kingdom."
>
> But Jesus answered, "You do not know what you are asking. Are you able to drink the cup that I am to drink?"
>
> They said to him, "We are able."
>
> He said to them, "You will drink my cup, but to sit at my right hand and at my left is not mine to grant, but it is for those for whom it has been prepared by my Father." (Matt. 20:20-23)

Clearly James and John—and their mother, who put them up to it—thought that Jesus was going to be the kind of king David was. And a king like that needs ministers, who, of course, would be rich and powerful.

It wasn't just James and John. The rest were very annoyed at those two, clearly thinking they were trying to take all the glory for themselves.

But Jesus took the opportunity to teach them a little about what his kingdom would be like.

> And when the ten heard it, they were indignant at the two brothers. But Jesus called them to him and said, "You know that the rulers of the Gentiles lord it over them, and their great men exercise authority over them. It shall not be so among you; but whoever would be great among you must be your servant, and whoever would be first among you must be your slave; even as the Son of man came not

to be served but to serve, and to give his life as a ransom for many." (Matt. 20:24-28)

When we think of the disciples of Jesus, we think mainly of those Twelve—the eleven who would go on to be founders of the Church, and the one who would betray Jesus.

They were all men from the lower classes—with the possible exception of one. Judas Iscariot was the man who handled the money for the group, so it's likely that he was more familiar with money than the rest. The rest, though, all worked for a living.

Most were from Galilee, too, which was another strike against them as far as the upper classes were concerned. Galileans were hicks with funny accents: we know because people waiting outside at the trial of "Jesus the Galilean" said to Peter, "Certainly you are also one of them, for your accent betrays you" (Matt. 26:73). You could tell a Galilean by the way he talked, and then you probably thought of the old saying: "Can anything good come out of Nazareth?" (John 1:46).

Those were the twelve men we remember as "the disciples," but Jesus had many other followers while he was alive. After Judas killed himself, Peter decided that Judas needed to be replaced. "So one of the men who have accompanied us during all the time that the Lord Jesus went in and out among us, beginning from the baptism of John until the day when he was taken up from us—one of these men must become with us a witness to his resurrection" (Acts 1:21-22). There was a pool of candidates who had been following Jesus since John baptized him and had stayed with him through the Crucifixion, Resurrection, and Ascension. Out of that group the apostles picked two who were well qualified and then "cast lots"—basically, they flipped a coin.

By the time Jesus was crucified, his followers numbered in the thousands. When he entered Jerusalem on what we call Palm Sunday, it seemed as though the whole city was filled with his followers.

Yet, less than a week later, where were they? Instead, there was a mob shouting, "Crucify him!"

What happened? Did the same people who shouted "Blessed is he who comes in the name of the Lord" on Sunday shout "Crucify him!" just a few days later (Matt. 21:9; Mark 15:13)?

No doubt there were some of the same people in both crowds. But it seems more likely that many of the poor and powerless who had followed Jesus were now cowering somewhere while the rich and powerful fomented a riot of their own. The priestly class had been well-schooled in the art of manipulating Pontius Pilate by this time. They seem to have rounded up a cooperative crowd. But we know there were still faithful followers of Jesus—they were just afraid to be seen when the Roman soldiers were in a crucifying mood. Even the Twelve had scattered, hiding themselves away. Of all the disciples, only John stood at the foot of the Cross.

Still, in our story, there is one man who isn't afraid to be there with John and Mary. Lew Wallace wrote Judah Ben-Hur into the scene. His riches and social position might have made it less dangerous for him than for others, but Wallace also took care to show us that Judah didn't care about danger. He had seen too much, suffered too much, to go back home and lock the door. So Judah witnesses the last moments of Jesus—and through him we do as well.

> The light in the eyes went out; slowly the crowned head sank upon the laboring breast. Ben-Hur thought the

struggle over; but the fainting soul recollected itself, so that he and those around him caught the other and last words, spoken in a low voice, as if to one listening close by:

"Father, into thy hands I commend my spirit."

A tremor shook the tortured body; there was a scream of fiercest anguish, and the mission and the earthly life were over at once. The heart, with all its love, was broken; for of that, O reader, the man died!

Ben-Hur went back to his friends, saying, simply, "It is over; he is dead."

In a space incredibly short the multitude was informed of the circumstance. No one repeated it aloud; there was a murmur which spread from the knoll in every direction; a murmur that was little more than a whispering, "He is dead! he is dead!" and that was all. The people had their wish; the Nazarene was dead; yet they stared at each other aghast. His blood was upon them! And while they stood staring at each other, the ground commenced to shake; each man took hold of his neighbor to support himself; in a twinkling the darkness disappeared, and the sun came out; and everybody, as with the same glance, beheld the crosses upon the hill all reeling drunken-like in the earthquake. They beheld all three of them; but the one in the center was arbitrary; it alone would be seen; and for that it seemed to extend itself upwards, and lift its burden, and swing it to and fro higher and higher in the blue of the sky. And every man among them who had jeered at the Nazarene; every one who had struck him; every one who had voted to crucify him; every one who had marched in the procession from the city; every one who had in his heart wished him dead, and they were as ten to one, felt that he was in some way individually singled out from the many, and that if he would live he must get away quickly as possible from that menace in the sky. They started to run; they ran with all their might; on horseback, and camels, and in chariots they ran, as well as on foot; but then as if it were mad at them for what they had done, and had taken up the cause of the unoffending and friendless dead, the earthquake pursued them, and tossed them about, and flung them down, and terrified them yet more by the horrible noise of great rocks grinding and rending beneath them. They beat their breasts and shrieked with fear. His blood was upon them! The home-bred and the foreign, priest and layman, beggar, Sadducee, Pharisee, were overtaken in the race, and tumbled about indiscriminately. If they called on the Lord, the outraged earth answered for him in fury, and dealt them all alike. It did not even know wherein the high-priest was better than his guilty brethren; overtaking him, it tripped him up also, and smirched the fringing of his robe, and filled the golden bells with sand, and his mouth with dust. He and his people were alike in the one thing at least—the blood of the Nazarene was upon them all!

When the sunlight broke upon the crucifixion, the mother of the Nazarene, the disciple, and the faithful women of Galilee, the centurion and his soldiers, and Ben-Hur and his party, were all who remained upon the hill. These had not time to observe the flight of the multitude; they were too loudly called upon to take care of themselves.

"Seat thyself here," said Ben-Hur to Esther, making a place for her at her father's feet. "Now cover thine eyes and look not up; but put thy trust in God, and the spirit of yon just man so foully slain."

"Nay," said Simonides, reverently, "let us henceforth speak of him as the Christ."

"Be it so," said Ben-Hur.[20]

[20] *Ben-Hur*, bk. 8, chap. 10.

6

Making Martyrs: Crime and Punishment

We're shocked by the brutality of the Roman soldiers who break up the Hur household in *Ben-Hur*. And we're certainly shocked by the brutality of crucifixion when we think about it.

But we shouldn't be. Brutality was the normal Roman response to crime—and not just to proven crime, but to suspected crime as well.

> He was leading her to the summer-house, when the roof jarred under their feet, and a crash of strong timbers being burst away, followed by a cry of surprise and agony, arose apparently from the court-yard below. He stopped and listened. The cry was repeated; then came a rush of many feet, and voices lifted in rage blent with voices in prayer; and then the screams of women in mortal terror. The soldiers had beaten in the north gate, and were in possession of the house. The terrible sense of being hunted smote him. His first impulse was to fly; but where? Nothing but wings would serve him. Tirzah, her eyes wild with fear, caught his arm.
>
> "O Judah, what does it mean?"
>
> The servants were being butchered—and his mother! Was not one of the voices he heard hers? With all the will

> left him, he said, "Stay here, and wait for me, Tirzah. I will go down and see what is the matter, and come back to you."
>
> His voice was not steady as he wished. She clung closer to him.
>
> Clearer, shriller, no longer a fancy, his mother's cry arose. He hesitated no longer.
>
> "Come, then, let us go."
>
> The terrace or gallery at the foot of the steps was crowded with soldiers. Other soldiers with drawn swords ran in and out of the chambers. At one place a number of women on their knees clung to each other or prayed for mercy. Apart from them, one with torn garments, and long hair streaming over her face, struggled to tear loose from a man all whose strength was tasked to keep his hold. Her cries were shrillest of all; cutting through the clamor, they had risen distinguishably to the roof. To her Judah sprang—his steps were long and swift, almost a winged flight—"Mother, mother!" he shouted. She stretched her hands towards him; but when almost touching them he was seized and forced aside. Then he heard some one say, speaking loudly,
>
> "That is he!"
>
> Judah looked, and saw—Messala.[21]

The movie version doesn't stray far from Lew Wallace's narrative in this scene. It doesn't have to. The scene is dramatic and appalling enough as Wallace wrote it—and sufficiently true to history. Roman soldiers coming upon a crime scene—especially

[21] Ibid., bk. 2, chap. 6.

one where one of the local populace had attacked a Roman official—would butcher first and ask questions later. And their questions would be posed in the form of torture. Not because they were cruel or angry, but because torture was simply the usual prescribed form of interrogation.

ᨏ

Remember how Pilate conducted his trial of Jesus.

> After he had said this, he went out to the Jews again, and told them, "I find no crime in him. But you have a custom that I should release one man for you at the Passover; will you have me release for you the King of the Jews?"
>
> They cried out again, "Not this man, but Barabbas!" Now Barabbas was a robber.
>
> Then Pilate took Jesus and scourged him. (John 18:38-40; 19:1)

Anyone used to the legal system in almost any nation on earth today will say, "Wait! What?"

Pilate has just told the people, "I find no crime in this man." Then he takes the man *whom he has called innocent* and scourges him.

Many innocent people are tortured and killed today. But if they are tortured or killed by representatives of the legal system, those representatives at least have the decency to *pretend* that the victims are guilty.

And scourging is not just a slap on the wrist. A scourge was a whip with sharp fragments tied into knots along its length; it was designed to reduce the victim to a bloody mess. The victim could easily die just from the loss of blood.

Meanwhile the soldiers have to have their fun.

> And the soldiers plaited a crown of thorns, and put it on his head, and arrayed him in a purple robe; they came up to him, saying, "Hail, King of the Jews!" and struck him with their hands. (John 19:2-3)

Remember again that this is a man who is not convicted of a crime. And we're not just talking about innocent until proven guilty here. This is a man whom Pilate has specifically declared innocent. Had he changed his mind?

No—because *after* the scourging and the smacking around by the soldiers, Pilate makes the *same declaration*.

> Pilate went out again, and said to them, "See, I am bringing him out to you, that you may know that I find no crime in him." So Jesus came out, wearing the crown of thorns and the purple robe. Pilate said to them, "Behold the man!" (cf. John 19:4-5)

So Pilate ordered the scourging, and allowed his soldiers to have their fun, all the while believing that Jesus was innocent of any crime.

The modern mind boggles at this idea. The idea of "innocent until proven guilty" has always been hard for mobs to swallow at times when emotions run high, so we can understand—even if we don't approve of it—when authorities hurry off to the punishment part of the program without going through the formalities of finding somebody guilty. But we have a hard time imagining the kind of thought that goes into torturing someone when we're sure he's innocent.

Keep that in mind as you read the rest of the account.

> When the chief priests and the officers saw him, they cried out, "Crucify him, crucify him!"

> Pilate said to them, "Take him yourselves and crucify him, for I find no crime in him."
>
> The Jews answered him, "We have a law, and by that law he ought to die, because he has made himself the Son of God."
>
> When Pilate heard these words, he was the more afraid; he entered the praetorium again and said to Jesus, "Where are you from?" But Jesus gave no answer. Pilate therefore said to him, "You will not speak to me? Do you not know that I have power to release you, and power to crucify you?"
>
> Jesus answered him, "You would have no power over me unless it had been given you from above; therefore he who delivered me to you has the greater sin."
>
> Upon this Pilate sought to release him, but the Jews cried out, "If you release this man, you are not Caesar's friend; every one who makes himself a king sets himself against Caesar." (John 19:6-12)

Anyone can see here that the priests are playing Pilate like a cheap violin. When did the chief priests become Caesar's best friends? They're just shamelessly manipulating Pilate, which is what they did for most of his reign. And it works. Pilate still doesn't want to kill Jesus, but the priests have won the battle. Pilate won't let it be said that he was a traitor to Caesar.

> When Pilate heard these words, he brought Jesus out and sat down on the judgment seat at a place called The Pavement, and in Hebrew, Gabbatha. Now it was the day of Preparation of the Passover; it was about the sixth hour. He said to the Jews, "Behold your King!"
>
> They cried out, "Away with him, away with him, crucify him!"

> Pilate said to them, "Shall I crucify your King?"
>
> The chief priests answered, "We have no king but Caesar."
>
> Then he handed him over to them to be crucified. (John 19:13-16)

It was typical of Pontius Pilate that he was weak when he most needed strength and was unbending when a little flexibility would have won friends and influenced people. Here he was convinced that Jesus of Nazareth was a harmless crank, but, sure, crucify him if you like.

Here in our century, we're horrified by the idea that someone in authority would scourge an innocent man. But that's because we all think like Christians now. We see each human being as infinitely valuable. To someone like Pilate, that statement would have been mystic nonsense. It would have been incomprehensible. Pilate could have told you exactly how much Jesus would be worth if you sold him as a slave, for example—a considerable amount, although rather less after he had been scourged a couple of times, but certainly not infinitely valuable.

The general principle of ancient law was that some people had power over other people, and some people were powerless.

There were degrees of power and powerlessness. A Roman citizen, for example, actually had rights. Jesus could not have been treated that way if he had been a Roman citizen. But Roman citizenship was a rare thing in first-century Judea. We're used to the idea that everyone can be a citizen of our country just by being born here, but Roman citizenship was a privilege of the few.

In the Acts of the Apostles, Luke tells us how Paul used his Roman citizenship—he was the only one of the apostles we know to have been a Roman citizen—to good effect when he was about to face just the same sort of treatment Pilate gave Jesus. Paul's preaching has caused yet another riot to break out in Jerusalem, and of course the Roman authorities step in to arrest him as the chief troublemaker.

> And as they cried out and waved their garments and threw dust into the air, the tribune commanded him to be brought into the barracks, and ordered him to be examined by scourging, to find out why they shouted thus against him.
>
> But when they had tied him up with the thongs, Paul said to the centurion who was standing by, "Is it lawful for you to scourge a man who is a Roman citizen, and uncondemned?"
>
> When the centurion heard that, he went to the tribune and said to him, "What are you about to do? For this man is a Roman citizen."
>
> So the tribune came and said to him, "Tell me, are you a Roman citizen?"
>
> And he said, "Yes."
>
> The tribune answered, "I bought this citizenship for a large sum."
>
> Paul said, "But I was born a citizen."
>
> So those who were about to examine him withdrew from him instantly; and the tribune also was afraid, for he realized that Paul was a Roman citizen and that he had bound him. (Acts 22:23-29)

The law said that the authorities could not scourge a Roman citizen unless he had actually been legally condemned to scourging. The Roman officials here know that they are in serious trouble if Paul complains about them to their superiors. But how could they have known he was a citizen? Roman citizenship was a rare and valuable thing—"I bought this citizenship for a large sum," says the tribune—and who would have expected some random troublemaker preaching in the synagogue to be a Roman citizen?

And if he had not been a Roman citizen, then what the officials were doing was not only legal but expected. It was standard procedure; they would have been negligent if they hadn't scourged Paul. Torture was the normal way of asking questions of anyone who was not a citizen. In fact, by what seems to us a bizarre principle of Roman legal theory, the testimony of a slave was not admissible in court *unless* he had been tortured. It was presumed that everything a slave said was a lie, perhaps told out of loyalty to his master. But pain could magically extract the truth.

Looked at this way, what Pilate did to Jesus was only part of the expected Roman interrogation process. Yes, Pilate found no crime in him, but he would be negligent in his duties if he didn't at least *look* for information. And the way you looked for information was through torture.

Suppose the accused was found guilty: he admitted his guilt under torture, or the magistrate was sufficiently convinced of his guilt by the evidence.

Then what?

One of the most important principles of Roman punishment was that the criminal should be an example to discourage crime. People should be able to see the punishment and say, "If I committed that crime, I would be in that man's place." And they should definitely not want to be in that man's place.

Making Martyrs: Crime and Punishment

The galley scenes in *Ben-Hur* vividly portray how horrible life as a galley convict would be—they're based on the actual experiences of convicts sent to the galleys in more modern times. If the Romans had used convicts to row their galleys, they would definitely have treated them that way. We know because of the way they treated convicts in other jobs. The convicts were whipped to make them work and whipped if they fell down exhausted. They were whipped if they collapsed from being whipped too much.

Forced labor was one way of making a convict useful. Convicts might be sent to the mines, for example—an unpleasant and dangerous job, possibly more deadly overall than service in the galleys. Today we spend millions on safety equipment, and mining is still dangerous; when the miners were condemned prisoners, there was no need for safety equipment at all.

Female convicts were often sent to the brothels. They could certainly be of some use there—after all, somebody had to do it. Because Christian women valued their purity, it was especially amusing for a judge to send Christians to the brothels. Many lives of the martyrs tell of Christian women who chose martyrdom rather than a life of forced prostitution.

But, of course, for extraordinary crimes the Romans wanted extraordinarily striking examples.

Crucifixion was a very striking example. It was reserved for the worst criminals—especially traitors who had rebelled against the state. A Roman citizen could not be crucified at all. One famous example: St. Peter and St. Paul were executed on the same day for the same crime. Peter was crucified, but Paul was beheaded. It was the last privilege of his Roman citizenship: no matter how vile they thought his crime was, the Romans couldn't crucify him.

Another way of setting a striking example was by making the condemned "perform" in the arena. Some prisoners might be forced to fight as gladiators. Others were forced to fight the beasts, which means that they were sent into the arena unarmed, and some exotic beast such as a leopard was invited to tear them to shreds. This was what the Romans had instead of reality TV.

Next to the chariot race, the galley scenes probably give us the most remembered images from *Ben-Hur*. Who can forget the burly man with the kettle drums, the constant lash of the whip, the slaves worked until they collapse and are thrown overboard? It's all so real, so vivid.

But it's actually all made up.

The galley scenes in *Ben-Hur* are a little bit of historical liberty. These days, almost all historians agree that the Roman navy used free men to row the galleys.

Part of the reason was simple economics. A slave—even one condemned to slavery for some crime—was a valuable possession. Buying a slave required a large initial investment. And what if he got killed in some naval battle? You would just have to write off that investment.[22]

No, it was far more economical to hire men to row the galleys. You could find men who were desperately poor and offer them a regular salary that was more than they could ever make in any other job. Then, if they died, you just stopped paying them. If

[22] Lionel Casson, *The Ancient Mariners* (Princeton: Princeton University Press, 1991), 87. Here he writes about the economics of the Athenian galleys in pre-Roman times, but the same arguments apply to Roman galleys.

they lived, they still probably wouldn't be in the job long enough for their pay to equal the price of a slave. The economics of slavery were all against slave labor in the military.

There was also the question of how effective slaves would be in a battle. In the great civil wars just before the birth of Christ, the combatants sometimes resorted to slaves when the supply of free oarsmen ran out—but the slaves were given their freedom first.

> When Augustus was desperately trying to build up his naval force to combat Sextus, he enlisted slaves as rowers—but he made certain to free them before sitting them on the benches; there were no slaves then or thereafter in the Roman navy.[23]

The theory was probably that the prospect of living free afterward would be a big motivation for the oarsmen, and motivated oarsmen win battles. In reality, it was only in the 1500s or so that it became common to send convicts to the galleys.

Nevertheless, the idea of sending criminals to the galleys fits very well with the spirit of Roman punishment. It seems true to life because it fits so well with everything else we know about the Roman world. It was probably military considerations that kept them from doing it, rather than any idea that it wouldn't be a fit punishment.

The Romans did not keep large prisons for incarcerating criminals. They had small jails for people awaiting trial—when Paul writes from prison, he is always writing as one awaiting trial, not as someone sentenced to prison. But to the Roman mind there was no point in incarceration after the trial. If the prisoner was

[23] Ibid., 88.

guilty, then either there was no more use for him, in which case he should die, or he owed the state something, and he should be useful.

So even if Wallace was wrong in the detail, he was right in the big picture. Whenever there was an exceptionally dangerous job to be done, the Romans were likely to have it done by prisoners.

It would be pleasant to say that Christianity brought humanity to the treatment of prisoners. But it would be only partially true. Christian emperors stopped the practice of throwing convicts to the beasts, and we have to give them credit for that. They also stopped the practice of crucifixion. But they certainly didn't completely end the use of prisoners in dangerous jobs where they weren't likely to survive very long.

On the other hand, even free men took on dangerous jobs in those days. And certainly one of the most dangerous jobs of all was rowing the galleys.

7

The Empire of Oceans: Ben-Hur's Imprisonment on the Sea

"The Romans are an anomaly in maritime history," wrote Lionel Casson, "a race of lubbers who became lords of the sea in spite of themselves."[24]

And this is the key to understanding the galley scenes in *Ben-Hur*. Romans did not like the sea, so Roman naval war was usually carried on as much like land war as possible. The strategy was to ram or grapple the enemy's ship, and then Roman soldiers would pour onto the deck and fight with swords the way they did on land.

Thus the galleys: it was vital that the Romans should be able to turn their ships quickly in battle to get them into ramming position, and only a galley with oars could do that.

Romans had sailing ships, of course, but they were not very good at maneuvering under sail. If there was to be a naval battle, the Romans always relied on oars, which could turn the ship in any direction regardless of what the wind happened to be doing. In fact, galleys were the usual warships in the Mediterranean right up into the 1700s, and for much the same reason: when

[24] Lionel Casson, *The Ancient Mariners*, chap. 12.

maneuverability was the key to winning the battle, you couldn't rely on the wind.

Big Roman ships had an enormous number of oars. A trireme was so called because it had three ranks of oars, one above the other. Those were big ships, but the Romans had bigger. Three banks of oars were probably the practical limit, but you could get more power by having multiple oarsmen on each oar. So there were quadriremes and quinqueremes, all the way up to monster ships with twenty or more ranks of oarsmen.

Wallace may have dropped the ball on the business of galley slaves, but he certainly knew his triremes. Remember what he told us: "Once I went to Washington, thence to Boston, for no purpose but to exhaust their libraries in an effort to satisfy myself of the mechanical arrangement of the oars in the interior of a trireme." It was typical of Wallace that he would hop on a train, not once but twice, because some little detail of history was eating at him, and he couldn't rest until he found the answer. The parts of his book that deal with the galleys are vividly real precisely because you can see every detail. Every movie version tries to match that vivid sense of dread and chaos under the deck that Wallace masterfully described when the *Astroea,* the ship in which Ben-Hur is a galley slave, heads into battle.

> Of the hundred and twenty slaves chained to the benches, not one but asked himself the question. They were without incentive. Patriotism, love of honor, sense of duty, brought them no inspiration. They felt the thrill common to men rushed helpless and blind into danger. It may be supposed the dullest of them, poising his oar, thought of all that might happen, yet could promise himself nothing; for victory would but rivet his chains the firmer, while the

chances of the ship were his; sinking or on fire, he was doomed to her fate.

Of the situation without they might not ask. And who were the enemy? And what if they were friends, brethren, countrymen? The reader, carrying the suggestion forward, will see the necessity which governed the Roman when, in such emergencies, he locked the hapless wretches to their seats.

There was little time, however, for such thought with them. A sound like the rowing of galleys astern attracted Ben-Hur, and the *Astroea* rocked as if in the midst of countering waves. The idea of a fleet at hand broke upon him—a fleet in manoeuvre—forming probably for attack. His blood started with the fancy.

Another signal came down from the deck. The oars dipped, and the galley started imperceptibly. No sound from without, none from within, yet each man in the cabin instinctively poised himself for a shock; the very ship seemed to catch the sense, and hold its breath, and go crouched tiger-like.

In such a situation time is inappreciable; so that Ben-Hur could form no judgment of distance gone. At last there was a sound of trumpets on deck, full, clear, long blown. The chief beat the sounding-board until it rang; the rowers reached forward full length, and, deepening the dip of their oars, pulled suddenly with all their united force. The galley, quivering in every timber, answered with a leap. Other trumpets joined in the clamor—all from the rear, none forward—from the latter quarter only a rising sound of voices in tumult heard briefly. There was a mighty blow; the rowers in front of the chief's platform reeled, some of them fell; the ship bounded back, recovered, and rushed on more irresistibly than before. Shrill and high arose the shrieks of men in terror; over the blare of trumpets, and the grind and crash of the collision, they arose; then under his feet, under the keel, pounding, rumbling, breaking to pieces, drowning, Ben-Hur felt something overridden. The men about him looked at each other afraid. A shout of triumph from the deck—the beak of the Roman had won! But who were they whom the sea had drunk? Of what tongue, from what land were they?

No pause, no stay! Forward rushed the *Astroea*; and, as it went, some sailors ran down, and plunging the cotton balls into the oil-tanks, tossed them dripping to comrades at the head of the stairs: fire was to be added to other horrors of the combat.

Directly the galley heeled over so far that the oarsmen on the uppermost side with difficulty kept their benches. Again the hearty Roman cheer, and with it despairing shrieks. An opposing vessel, caught by the grappling-hooks of the great crane swinging from the prow, was being lifted into the air that it might be dropped and sunk.

The shouting increased on the right hand and on the left; before, behind, swelled an indescribable clamor. Occasionally there was a crash, followed by sudden peals of fright, telling of other ships ridden down, and their crews drowned in the vortexes.

Nor was the fight all on one side. Now and then a Roman in armor was borne down the hatchway, and laid bleeding, sometimes dying, on the floor.

Sometimes, also, puffs of smoke, blended with steam, and foul with the scent of roasting human flesh, poured into the cabin, turning the dimming light into yellow murk. Gasping for breath the while, Ben-Hur knew they were passing through the cloud of a ship on fire, and burning up with the rowers chained to the benches.

The *Astroea* all this time was in motion. Suddenly she stopped. The oars forward were dashed from the hands of the rowers, and the rowers from their benches. On deck, then, a furious trampling, and on the sides a grinding of ships afoul of each other. For the first time the beating of the gavel was lost in the uproar. Men sank on the floor in fear or looked about seeking a hiding-place. In the midst of the panic a body plunged or was pitched headlong down the hatchway, falling near Ben-Hur. He beheld the half-naked carcass, a mass of hair blackening the face, and under it a shield of bull-hide and wicker-work—a barbarian from the white-skinned nations of the North whom death had robbed of plunder and revenge. How came he there? An iron hand had snatched him from the opposing deck—no, the *Astroea* had been boarded! The Romans were fighting on their own deck? The tumult thundered above him; he looked around; in the cabin all was confusion—the rowers on the benches paralyzed; men running blindly hither and thither; only the chief on his seat imperturbable, vainly beating the sounding-board, and waiting the orders of the tribune—in the red murk illustrating the matchless discipline which had won the world.[25]

[25] *Ben-Hur*, bk. 3, chap. 5.

Wallace knew better than almost any other novelist what the confusion of battle was like. He knew that the real horror of it, psychologically, is the not knowing. Wherever you are in the battle, you know only what is going on immediately around you. What is happening with the rest of the battle? Who is winning? What do the sounds from near and far mean? These are things you cannot know.

And if that is true for any soldier, even a general in the Union Army, imagine how much more so it is for the men at the oars in a Roman galley. Slaves or not, they have almost no knowledge of what is happening above on the deck, let alone on other ships. They can only guess from the sudden shocks and terrible sounds what might be happening around them. Slaves or not, they were not in an enviable position.

Romans used sailing ships for much of their ordinary transportation, but even large merchant ships might be rowed galleys. That was because sailing was a very unreliable way of getting anywhere. If it was important to get there fast, you needed a galley. If it was important to be able to maneuver quickly once you got there, you needed a galley.

In spite of their sophistication in most other sciences, Romans were rather primitive sailors. Their ships could sail with the wind or at a bit of an angle to the wind, but in general if the wind was blowing in the wrong direction, they were stuck. They had to wait until the wind changed. A medieval Viking ship could literally have sailed rings around any Roman sailing ship.

When the wind did let them sail, Roman sailors usually hugged the coastline as much as they could. The Mediterranean—which the Romans called Mare Nostrum, "Our Sea"—was known so well that sailors might strike out into open water. But even there they were cautious. And with good reason: weather in the Mediterranean can suddenly turn very vicious. The floor of the Mediterranean is littered with ancient wrecks—priceless treasures for archaeologists today, which is no consolation at all to the sailors who went down with those ships.

The most vivid and exciting sea story to survive from the Roman period is actually in your Bible. In the Acts of the Apostles, Luke tells what happened when it was decided that Paul, now a prisoner, should be taken to Rome for his appeal. Luke tells this story in the first person plural: "we put out to sea," not "they put out to sea." Most biblical scholars agree that he tells it that way because he himself was on the ship, traveling with Paul and his companions. What we have in Acts 27, then, is an eyewitness account of a Roman sailing voyage that went catastrophically wrong.

> When it was decided that we should sail to Italy, they handed Paul and some other prisoners over to a centurion named Julius of the Cohort Augusta. We went on board a ship from Adramyttium bound for ports in the province of Asia and set sail. Aristarchus, a Macedonian from Thessalonica, was with us. On the following day we put in at Sidon where Julius was kind enough to allow Paul to visit his friends who took care of him. From there we put out to sea and sailed around the sheltered side of Cyprus because of the headwinds, and crossing the open sea off the coast of Cilicia and Pamphylia we came to Myra in Lycia.
>
> There the centurion found an Alexandrian ship that was sailing to Italy and put us on board.

> For many days we made little headway, arriving at Cnidus only with difficulty, and because the wind would not permit us to continue our course we sailed for the sheltered side of Crete off Salmone. We sailed past it with difficulty and reached a place called Fair Havens, near which was the city of Lasea. (Acts 27:1-8)

You notice immediately how much the sailors are at the mercy of the wind. They can't go against it; they can only make for a port as best they can and hope for the wind to change. In this case, the delay was costly: first in one ship and then in another, Paul's captors had wasted so much time with unfavorable winds that it was now past what most people considered the safe sailing season in the Mediterranean.

If you look at a map of the Mediterranean, you can see that Crete is only about halfway to Italy, and perhaps a third of the way to Rome.

> As much time had been lost, and the voyage was already dangerous because the fast[26] had already gone by, Paul advised them, "Sirs, I perceive that the voyage will be with injury and much loss, not only of the cargo and the ship, but also of our lives."
>
> But the centurion paid more attention to the captain and to the owner of the ship than to what Paul said. And because the harbor was not suitable to winter in, the majority advised to put to sea from there, on the chance that somehow they could reach Phoenix, a harbor of

[26] Yom Kippur, the Day of Atonement, which came at about the end of the season Mediterranean sailors considered safe for traveling.

> Crete, looking northeast and southeast, and winter there. (Acts 27:9-11)

The plan was to go a short distance to a safer port, still on the island of Crete, and spend the winter there. It was a big mistake.

> And when the south wind blew gently, supposing that they had obtained their purpose, they weighed anchor and sailed along Crete, close inshore. But soon a tempestuous wind, called the northeaster, struck down from the land; and when the ship was caught and could not face the wind, we gave way to it and were driven. And running under the lee of a small island called Cauda, we managed with difficulty to secure the boat; after hoisting it up, they took measures to undergird the ship; then, fearing that they should run on the Syrtis, they lowered the gear, and so were driven. As we were violently storm-tossed, they began next day to throw the cargo overboard; and the third day they cast out with their own hands the tackle of the ship. And when neither sun nor stars appeared for many a day, and no small tempest lay on us, all hope of our being saved was at last abandoned. (Acts 27:13-20)

When the ship is in danger of being overwhelmed by the sea, you throw things overboard to lighten it. A lighter ship rises higher in the water, putting the deck higher above the pounding waves. First, the cargo goes, but then you start to look for other things to throw overboard. If you're throwing away the ship's tackle—the equipment you use for controlling the ship—you have to be pretty desperate.

> As they had been long without food, Paul then came forward among them and said, "Men, you should have

> listened to me, and should not have set sail from Crete and incurred this injury and loss. I now bid you take heart; for there will be no loss of life among you, but only of the ship. For this very night there stood by me an angel of the God to whom I belong and whom I worship, and he said, 'Do not be afraid, Paul; you must stand before Caesar; and lo, God has granted you all those who sail with you.' So take heart, men, for I have faith in God that it will be exactly as I have been told. But we shall have to run on some island."
>
> When the fourteenth night had come, as we were drifting across the sea of Adria, about midnight the sailors suspected that they were nearing land. So they sounded and found twenty fathoms; a little farther on they sounded again and found fifteen fathoms. And fearing that we might run on the rocks, they let out four anchors from the stern, and prayed for day to come.
>
> And as the sailors were seeking to escape from the ship, and had lowered the boat into the sea, under pretense of laying out anchors from the bow, Paul said to the centurion and the soldiers, "Unless these men stay in the ship, you cannot be saved." Then the soldiers cut away the ropes of the boat, and let it go. (Acts 27:21-32)

At this point, not surprisingly, the sailors are desperate. They figure they can just abandon the soldiers and prisoners to their fate—which shows us how much regard they had for Roman soldiers. Probably the sailors felt pretty much the way everyone in the provinces felt about Roman soldiers: they were at best a necessary evil, a constant source of low-level resentment. Knowing that they can't expect any loyalty from the sailors, the soldiers get rid of the one lifeboat on the ship. It's the only way to keep the sailors on board.

> As day was about to dawn, Paul urged them all to take some food, saying, "Today is the fourteenth day that you have continued in suspense and without food, having taken nothing. Therefore I urge you to take some food; it will give you strength, since not a hair is to perish from the head of any of you." And when he had said this, he took bread, and giving thanks to God in the presence of all he broke it and began to eat.
>
> Then they all were encouraged and ate some food themselves. (We were in all two hundred and seventy-six persons in the ship.) And when they had eaten enough, they lightened the ship, throwing out the wheat into the sea.
>
> Now when it was day, they did not recognize the land, but they noticed a bay with a beach, on which they planned if possible to bring the ship ashore. So they cast off the anchors and left them in the sea, at the same time loosening the ropes that tied the rudders; then hoisting the foresail to the wind they made for the beach. But striking a shoal they ran the vessel aground; the bow stuck and remained immovable, and the stern was broken up by the surf.
>
> The soldiers' plan was to kill the prisoners, lest any should swim away and escape; but the centurion, wishing to save Paul, kept them from carrying out their purpose. He ordered those who could swim to throw themselves overboard first and make for the land, and the rest on planks or on pieces of the ship. And so it was that all escaped to land. (Acts 27:33-44)

You'll notice, in these last few lines, the typical Roman attitude toward prisoners. Remember that Paul at the time was not a convicted criminal: he was using his right as a Roman citizen to make an appeal to the emperor, and that was why he was on the way to Rome. Nevertheless, the soldiers thought—and most Romans would have said they were quite correct—that it was better for suspected criminals to be killed rather than allowed to escape.

It's obvious from the story in Acts that the great problem for Roman shipping was maneuverability. The sailors were powerless when the wind was blowing the wrong way. That was why warships were galleys: it was expensive to employ all those men to row, but it was the only way a ship could maneuver well enough to be useful in battle. A Roman galley could almost literally turn in place by carefully coordinated rowing.

There were serious limitations to the galleys. They were built for lightness and speed, since maneuvering was key to almost every naval strategy. But that made them vulnerable. In the open sea they were useless, easily overwhelmed by the waves. In the wars against Carthage, Rome more than once lost almost her entire navy in a single storm.

So the usual method of navigating the galleys was to hug the shoreline even more closely than an ordinary Roman sailor would do. At night, the galleys would be beached, and the men would set up a hurriedly improvised camp. They would probably have to forage for food or steal it from the locals, because there was very little room for supplies on the galleys. They were specialized for speed and carrying soldiers: above decks the soldiers and their weapons took up most of the room, and the space below the deck was filled with massive oars.

Manning those oars was a rotten job. The men who did it were paid well, which was the inducement that persuaded them to sign on. Most of them were poor—too poor to afford the equipment that an ordinary soldier had to provide for himself, which was why they signed up for rowing duty instead.

Poor or not, though, they were skilled workers. Lew Wallace gives us some idea of the kind of expertise it took to synchronize the movements of the oars. A good crew could turn a ship on a dime. That took lots of training, which meant that—poor or not—the skilled oarsman represented a big investment for the Roman navy.

In the war against Carthage, when Rome suddenly found herself forced to become a naval power, the Romans went all out and built up a huge navy in an incredibly short time. But building the ships was only part of the preparation: they had to build up crews of oarsmen to man them. Farmers and peasants who had never seen the sea were pressed into service—but how to train them when the ships were still under construction? The answer was almost as amazing as the ship-construction program itself. The Romans built life-size galley simulators on land—hastily constructed rowing frames where the new recruits could be drilled with real oars, learning to synchronize their movements on command.[27] It worked: the Roman navy won stunning victories over the practiced Carthaginians, who until that time had ruled the western Mediterranean unopposed.

Ramming was a big part of Roman naval strategy. If you could maneuver just right, you had a good chance of taking out a whole enemy galley with one blow. Then your oarsmen would reverse with all their might, and—with any luck—your

[27] Casson, *The Ancient Mariners*, 145.

own galley would be clear of the wreckage before the other one went down. Each galley was fitted with an enormous bronze ram, cast all in one piece. The size of these castings was huge even by today's standards—a modern factory might be reluctant to undertake them.

But it was also good to capture enemy galleys intact, because you could both use them and imitate their technology. One of the clever inventions the Romans added to naval warfare was the "raven," which came as quite a surprise the first time it was used against the Carthaginian navy. It was an elegantly simple idea; the scholar Lionel Casson suggests that it might have been invented by the famous Archimedes, whose adopted city of Syracuse was a Roman ally at the time.[28]

The raven was a four-foot-wide plank with a heavy spike at the end, attached to a pole in the bow of the ship. The Roman galley would rush toward an enemy ship; then the ropes that held the plank of the raven were let out, and with a crunch the plank would swing down, burying its spike in the enemy's deck. Immediately Roman soldiers would pour across the plank, fighting hand to hand just the way they would on land. That gave the Romans a huge advantage, because on land they were the most disciplined fighters in the world. We can imagine that the raven might have been getting a workout in the galley scene in *Ben-Hur*.

In the very large galleys, where there were multiple men to each oar, only one of the men on each oar had to be an expert. He set the pace; the rest were there to add muscle. That meant oarsmen could be recruited more hastily and put into service with less training.

[28] Ibid., 146.

In fact, they could even be slaves, freed just for that purpose.

And since we bring up the subject, what would life have been like for those freed slaves if they survived the battle?

8

Roman Slavery: Bondage, Property, and Punishment

To deal with the story of *Ben-Hur*, we have to think of how to deal with slavery. The Hur family keeps slaves. Judah Ben-Hur himself is made a slave. His love interest and future wife, Esther, is a slave. The institution of slavery pervades *Ben-Hur*, because it pervaded Roman society, and indeed the whole ancient world. There was not an ancient civilization that did not recognize some people as owned by others.

Most Americans think first of the southern United States when they think of slavery. But slavery was very different there from what it was in ancient Rome. In both places, slavery involved one human being owning another. But in the United States, slaves were exclusively African. The difference in physical appearance usually made it easy to tell who was supposed to be a slave and who was not; there were some free Africans in the South, but very few. At the height of the slave economy before the Civil War, all sorts of laws were in place to make sure that slaves could never win their freedom.

In the Roman Empire, on the other hand, it was a very common thing for a slave to earn enough money to buy his freedom. It was also a very common thing for a free person to become a slave, either because his country was conquered or because he committed a crime whose punishment was slavery. There was no obvious physical difference that made one person a slave and another free. There were huge numbers of slaves, but there were also large numbers of freedmen—former slaves who had bought or been given their freedom.

Slavery was a fact throughout the ancient world. The Romans certainly didn't invent it. The ancient Israelites were slaves in Egypt, and then when they were freed and began to prosper, they kept slaves of their own. The Law of Moses made provisions for slavery, as it did for everything else that was a fact of life. One rule the Israelites had that was different from the condition of slaves in most of the world was that Hebrew slaves, at least, could not be kept indefinitely without their consent. A slave had to be released after six years of service—unless he decided of his own free will that he would stay in his master's household.

> If your brother, a Hebrew man, or a Hebrew woman, is sold to you, he shall serve you six years, and in the seventh year you shall let him go free from you. And when you let him go free from you, you shall not let him go empty-handed; you shall furnish him liberally out of your flock, out of your threshing floor, and out of your wine press; as the LORD your God has blessed you, you shall give to him. You shall remember that you were a slave in the land of Egypt, and the LORD your God redeemed you; therefore I command you this today.
>
> But if he says to you, "I will not go out from you," because he loves you and your household, since he fares well with you, then you shall take an awl, and thrust

> it through his ear into the door, and he shall be your bondman for ever. And to your bondwoman you shall do likewise.
>
> It shall not seem hard to you, when you let him go free from you; for at half the cost of a hired servant he has served you six years. So the LORD your God will bless you in all that you do. (Deut. 15:12-18)

This passage from Deuteronomy repeats the law on slavery from Leviticus—but it is only Deuteronomy that adds that last bit of advice, "It shall not seem hard to you."

In Lew Wallace's novel, the Hur family slave Simonides is one of those slaves who decided to stay with the household.

> "My father and mother were Hebrew bond-servants, tenders of the fig and olive trees growing, with many vines, in the King's Garden hard by Siloam; and in my boyhood I helped them. They were of the class bound to serve forever. They sold me to the Prince Hur, then, next to Herod the King, the richest man in Jerusalem. From the garden he transferred me to his storehouse in Alexandria of Egypt, where I came of age. I served him six years, and in the seventh, by the law of Moses, I went free."

But Simonides fell in love with a slave in the Hur household. The prince, Judah's father, offered to free her as well, but she was happy where she was.

> "She would be my wife, she all the time said, if I would become her fellow in servitude. Our father Jacob served yet other seven years for his Rachel. Could I not as much for mine? But thy mother said I must become as she, to

serve forever. I came away, but went back. Look, Esther, look here."

He pulled out the lobe of his left ear.

"See you not the scar of the awl?"

"I see it," she said; "and, oh, I see how thou didst love my mother!"

"Love her, Esther! She was to me more than the Shulamite to the singing king, fairer, more spotless; a fountain of gardens, a well of living waters, and streams from Lebanon. The master, even as I required him, took me to the judges, and back to his door, and thrust the awl through my ear into the door, and I was his servant forever. So I won my Rachel. And was ever love like mine?"[29]

Slaves made up a large part of the population of the Roman Empire. No one knows exactly how large a part, and it seems to have varied considerably from one province to another. But wherever you went, there were slaves.

In Roman comedy, slaves were often the starring comedians, the characters who got the big laughs. They were usually schemers who had one desire: to earn their freedom. In that quest they would do absolutely anything; but in comedy, it usually turned out that the slave's schemes benefited his master, so that there were happy endings all around, and the slave was free. Sometimes, in fact, the slave would be in a position to be demanding.

[29] *Ben-Hur*, bk. 4, chap. 4.

Roman Slavery

In Plautus's comedy *Epidicus*, the title character is a slave whose schemes spiral into farcical complications. But in the end he manages to reunite his master with his long-lost daughter. Epidicus relishes the revelation: his master has bound his hands in preparation for a severe punishment and then discovers that Epidicus has done him the greatest service he could possibly do. Suddenly the tables are turned: even with his hands bound, Epidicus has all the power in the scene. He's not just going to be free: he's going to be free on his own terms.

> PERIPHANES. I find he has well deserved; and I'll take care / He shall not lose his recompense. Hold out / Your hands, that I may loose them.
>
> EPIDICUS. Touch me not.
>
> PERIPHANES. Hold them out then.
>
> EPIDICUS. Not I.
>
> PERIPHANES. You are to blame.
>
> EPIDICUS. Not till you've given me what I deserve.
>
> PERIPHANES. You ask no more than what is just and right. / A pair of sandals, vest, and cloak are yours.
>
> EPIDICUS. What else?
>
> PERIPHANES. Your freedom.
>
> EPIDICUS. Yes, and something more. / A new-made freedman ought to have enough / To eat as well.
>
> PERIPHANES. No more: it shall be done. / I'll give you a meal's meat.
>
> EPIDICUS. By Hercules! You shan't unbind me, till you've asked my pardon.
>
> PERIPHANES. If I unwittingly have done you wrong, / Honest Epidicus, I ask your pardon — / And so — I make you free —

Epidicus. I pardon you—/But 'tis against the grain—of pure necessity—/Here are my hands, unbind them when you please.[30]

We learn a lot about the complicated attitude toward slavery in ancient Rome from this little scene. On the one hand, slaves were recognized as property, and the master had absolute power over them—even the power of life and death. On the other hand, the instinct that recognized a slave as a human being could not be suppressed. The audiences who watched the Roman comedies loved to see slaves tricking their way to freedom. They rooted for the slave all the way through, and when he won his freedom at last, the play was over, because it had reached its obvious goal.

That ambiguous attitude was reflected in the wide spectrum of conditions of different kinds of slaves. Slaves could be brutally ill-treated or be pampered pets. Some slaves worked in agricultural jobs and had short and miserable lives. Some educated slaves were tutors for rich aristocrats' sons and lived as part of the family. And slaves could be anywhere on the spectrum between.

A slave who was well educated might be allowed to accumulate his own property: technically it belonged to his master, but he could be given complete control of it, and could even use it to buy his freedom. A master would often free his favorite slaves in his will, ensuring that there would be at least one group of people who remembered him fondly. A slave who rendered some important service to his master—such as, for example, saving him

[30] Plautus, *Epidicus*. Adapted from an anonymous blank-verse translation (London: T. Becket and P. A. de Hondt, 1772).

from drowning—might be freed as a reward and even adopted as a son. That is what happens in Lew Wallace's novel, where Judah saves Arrius, the commander of the fleet and is adopted as his son. (The movie had to simplify the plot of the sprawling book to make it short enough to watch in one sitting.)

Freed slaves fell into a special class of people in Roman law, almost but not quite as good as regular citizens. They could not hold certain offices, and they could not become senators. On the other hand, their children would be born free citizens, with no restrictions on their rights.

Of course, the upper classes looked down on freedmen. But that was not necessarily much of a detriment to a freedman with ambition. Some freedmen grew filthy rich precisely because they were not accepted in the upper ranks of Roman society. A Roman noble would not soil his hands with useful labor; a freedman could found a successful business and build it up into a giant commercial empire. (In Wallace's novel, this is what happens to Simonides, the father of Esther. In the necessarily simplified movie plot, he meets a different fate.) These nouveau-riche ex-slaves were the butts of constant jokes from the aristocracy, but they probably didn't care very much. They threw their money around like rap stars or big-league sports heroes, and money bought them all the respect they needed.

The satirist Petronius wrote what is certainly the most famous description of one of these rich freedmen in his *Satyricon*, a rambling novel whose most famous scene is Trimalchio's dinner party. The hero and narrator describes the paintings he saw on entering Trimalchio's lavish villa, one of which gives a complete visual biography of the master of the house:

> One of these paintings represented a slave-market, the men standing up with labels round their necks, while in another Trimalchio himself, wearing long hair, holding a caduceus in his hand and led by Minerva, was entering Rome. Further on, the ingenious painter had shown him learning accounts, and presently made steward of the estate, each incident being made clear by explanatory inscriptions. Lastly at the extreme end of the portico, Mercury was lifting the hero by the chin and placing him on the highest seat of a tribunal. Fortune stood by with her cornucopia, and the three Fates, spinning his destiny with a golden thread.[31]

In his entry hall, Trimalchio proudly displays the story of his life. He is bought at a slave market and brought to Rome; he becomes manager of his master's estate; finally, freed, he becomes Fortune's favorite. It's a lavish and tasteless display that only hints at the lavish bad taste to come in his little dinner party.

Petronius, the writer, earned the nickname Arbiter because he was considered the final authority on good taste. He recognized bad taste when he saw it, and bad taste was a rich freedman throwing money around. Aristocrats from old families could spend money on lavish parties, and Petronius would be happy to help them: in fact, he was the emperor Nero's favorite party planner, until Nero turned against him the way he turned against all his other favorites. Not waiting for Nero's death sentence, Petronius committed suicide in the most tasteful possible way,

[31] Petronius, *Satyricon*, chap. 5. Adapted from an anonymous translation often attributed (probably spuriously) to Oscar Wilde (Paris: Charles Carrington, 1902).

inviting a few friends over for a party and talking about amusing and trivial things while he opened his veins and slowly bled to death.

ஃ

By now we know something about how Romans and Israelites thought about slaves. But how did Christians deal with the question of slavery?

Since slavery was a fact of life throughout the world, it's not surprising that Christian writers didn't generally condemn it outright. But they did preach a fundamental revolution in the way people thought about slaves. A slave was a person—and merely to say that was to say something that rocked the foundations of the institution. "There is neither Jew nor Greek, there is neither slave nor free, there is neither male nor female; for you are all one in Christ Jesus" (Gal. 3:28). In one sentence, Paul lobbed three sticks of dynamite at everyone's assumptions about how the world worked.

Christian writers usually advised slaves to serve their masters well. And they usually advised the masters to treat slaves like brothers. If they discussed slavery as an idea, they tended to see it as one of the many undesirable consequences of original sin.

Paul's shortest letter in the New Testament perfectly illustrates the complicated early Christian attitude to slavery. A bit of setup: a slave named Onesimus—the name means "useful"—escaped from Philemon, a Christian master whom Paul knew. Somehow Paul met Onesimus and persuaded him to go back to his master.

It took a huge amount of courage for Onesimus to go back. A runaway slave could be punished in any way the master felt appropriate, up to and including death. But he did go back—bearing a letter from Paul, in which Paul implored Philemon to treat him kindly.

In fact, Paul asks for more than that. He does not *demand* that Philemon free Onesimus, but he drops none-too-subtle hints. Paul promises to pay back anything Onesimus might have stolen, although—again—he drops the completely unsubtle hint that Philemon owes Paul a debt he can never repay.

> Accordingly, though I am bold enough in Christ to command you to do what is required, yet for love's sake I prefer to appeal to you—I, Paul, an ambassador and now a prisoner also for Christ Jesus—I appeal to you for my child, Onesimus, whose father I have become in my imprisonment. (Formerly he was useless to you, but now he is indeed useful to you and to me.) I am sending him back to you, sending my very heart. I would have been glad to keep him with me, in order that he might serve me on your behalf during my imprisonment for the gospel; but I preferred to do nothing without your consent in order that your goodness might not be by compulsion but of your own free will.
>
> Perhaps this is why he was parted from you for a while, that you might have him back for ever, no longer as a slave but more than a slave, as a beloved brother, especially to me but how much more to you, both in the flesh and in the Lord. So if you consider me your partner, receive him as you would receive me. If he has wronged you at all, or owes you anything, charge that to my account. I, Paul, write this with my own hand, I will repay it—to say nothing of your owing me even your own self.

> Yes, brother, I want some benefit from you in the Lord. Refresh my heart in Christ.
>
> Confident of your obedience, I write to you, knowing that you will do even more than I say. (Philem. 8-21)

So what happened? Did Philemon free Onesimus when he got that letter? We don't know for certain, but we do know that there was a bishop of Ephesus named Onesimus in the early Church, one who was just the right age to be the former slave Paul had sent back to his master.

If Philemon did free his slave, he was not alone. Many Christians freed their slaves, and many freed slaves went on to become bishops in the Church. More than one of the early popes had been a slave.

Acceptance of slavery as a fact of life certainly wasn't a universal attitude. St. Gregory of Nyssa believed that it was quite simply impossible for a Christian to believe that all human beings were equal and at the same time keep slaves. But he didn't end slavery with his sermons.

What did change, though, was the way the law saw slaves—and this was much more of a revolution than we probably realize. Slaves had been merely property; now they were persons. A Roman of Augustus's time could buy a female slave for his sexual amusement; by the time of the Christian emperor Theodosius, a slave who was raped was automatically freed. No longer did the master have absolute rights over the bodies and lives of his slaves. He had to acknowledge that there were certain things he could not demand of them and certain rights they kept to themselves, because—in the eyes of God—they were human beings as much as he was.

And that in itself was a revolution.

9

Quarantine and Exile: Dealing with the Unclean

Separated from his mother and sister, Judah Ben-Hur can't live without knowing what has happened to them. Did they die right away? Are they still alive somewhere, living in poverty?

The discovery he makes is more appalling than he can imagine. They have been kept in a forgotten prison, and while there, they were attacked by the one disease the ancient world feared most: leprosy.

As with everything else, Lew Wallace did his research on leprosy. In his version of the story, there is a heartbreaking scene in which Judah's mother and sister catch a glimpse of him back in Jerusalem, while he reunites with the family's faithful old servant Amrah. But they cannot reveal themselves. Much as they long for the reunion, they will not take the risk that Judah, too, could contract leprosy.

> The spectators across the street heard a low exclamation, and saw the woman rub her eyes as if to renew their power, bend closer down, clasp her hands, gaze wildly around, look at the sleeper, stoop and raise the outlying hand,

and kiss it fondly—that which they wished so mightily to do, but dared not.

Awakened by the action, Ben-Hur instinctively withdrew the hand; as he did so, his eyes met the woman's.

"Amrah! O Amrah, is it thou?" he said.

The good heart made no answer in words, but fell upon his neck, crying for joy.

Gently he put her arms away, and lifting the dark face wet with tears, kissed it, his joy only a little less than hers. Then those across the way heard him say,

"Mother—Tirzah—O Amrah, tell me of them! Speak, speak, I pray thee!"

Amrah only cried afresh.

"Thou has seen them, Amrah. Thou knowest where they are; tell me they are at home."

Tirzah moved, but her mother, divining her purpose, caught her and whispered, "Do not go—not for life. Unclean, unclean!"

Her love was in tyrannical mood. Though both their hearts broke, he should not become what they were; and she conquered.

Meantime, Amrah, so entreated, only wept the more.

"Wert thou going in?" he asked, presently, seeing the board swung back. "Come, then. I will go with thee." He arose as he spoke. "The Romans—be the curse of the Lord upon them!—the Romans lied. The house is mine. Rise, Amrah, and let us go in."

A moment and they were gone, leaving the two in the shade to behold the gate staring blankly at them—the gate which they might not ever enter more. They nestled together in the dust.

> They had done their duty.
>
> Their love was proven.
>
> Next morning they were found, and driven out the city with stones.
>
> "Begone! Ye are of the dead; go to the dead!"
>
> With the doom ringing in their ears, they went forth.[32]

Driven out of the city with stones! Just because they had a disease? Is that really the way sick people were treated in those days?

Yes, it was. In fact, the Law of Moses has very strict rules about separating people with leprosy from the rest of the population. Every ancient people had similar laws.

The thirteenth chapter of Leviticus is a complete instruction manual for dealing with leprosy—a term that, in Hebrew, included a number of diseases of the skin. It describes all kinds of symptoms, telling the priests how to determine which ones are leprosy and which are not:

> When a man has on the skin of his body a swelling or an eruption or a spot, and it turns into a leprous disease on the skin of his body, then he shall be brought to Aaron the priest or to one of his sons the priests, and the priest shall examine the diseased spot on the skin of his body; and if the hair in the diseased spot has turned white and the disease appears to be deeper than the skin of his body, it is a leprous disease; when the priest has examined him he shall pronounce him unclean.
>
> But if the spot is white in the skin of his body, and appears no deeper than the skin, and the hair in it has not

[32] *Ben-Hur*, bk. 6, chap. 4.

> turned white, the priest shall shut up the diseased person for seven days; and the priest shall examine him on the seventh day, and if in his eyes the disease is checked and the disease has not spread in the skin, then the priest shall shut him up seven days more; and the priest shall examine him again on the seventh day, and if the diseased spot is dim and the disease has not spread in the skin, then the priest shall pronounce him clean; it is only an eruption; and he shall wash his clothes, and be clean.
>
> But if the eruption spreads in the skin, after he has shown himself to the priest for his cleansing, he shall appear again before the priest; and the priest shall make an examination, and if the eruption has spread in the skin, then the priest shall pronounce him unclean; it is leprosy. (Lev. 13:2-8)

This is only a small part of the chapter. It goes into minute medical detail. And so it must, because the consequences of being declared "unclean" are dire:

> The leper who has the disease shall wear torn clothes and let the hair of his head hang loose, and he shall cover his upper lip and cry, "Unclean, unclean." He shall remain unclean as long as he has the disease; he is unclean; he shall dwell alone in a habitation outside the camp. (Lev. 13:45-46)

Not only can a leper not live with other humans, but he can't even pretend to be human. He always must wear the uniform of a leper, so that he is instantly recognizable. He must broadcast the warning that he is a leper whenever he comes anywhere near another human being.

It all seems cruel, but for the sake of protecting the community, it makes sense. Leprosy is not a terribly contagious disease, like measles. But it is contagious: someone who spends a lot of time around people with leprosy is likely to get it eventually. There was no cure, and leprosy was a sentence to a very slow and painful death. So what do you do about that? You isolate the disease as much as possible in an attempt to make sure it doesn't spread. As a matter of public health, it's a sensible precaution.

But, of course, there is more than health involved. People with leprosy had been sentenced to a horrible fate: why would a just God do something like that? It must have been something the lepers did—some sin they committed. God must be punishing them. And if God was punishing them, the punishment had to be just. Therefore, leprosy was not just a disease: it was a sign of moral evil. The stigma was so strong that it persists even today, when we know how to cure leprosy. It's why people don't use the term *leper* anymore—because that word absorbed all the moral stigma attached to the disease by ignorant fear.

That sense of deserved punishment coupled with fear of the disease itself could make the treatment of people with leprosy very cruel. Wallace didn't exaggerate it a bit: lepers might be chased out of town with stones. They were already dead, as far as the society of the living was concerned.

But then there was Jesus of Nazareth.

Jesus did not chase anyone away. And people with all kinds of incurable diseases surrounded him wherever he went.

The cure of Judah's mother and sister happens a little differently in Wallace's version from the way it happens in the movie. In the novel, the cure comes from a direct meeting with Jesus the Christ on Palm Sunday.

Then at sight of the procession in the west, the thousands from the city halted, and began to wave their green branches, shouting, or rather chanting (for it was all in one voice),

"Blessed is the King of Israel that cometh in the name of the Lord!"

And all the thousands who were of the rider's company, both those near and those afar, replied so the air shook with the sound, which was as a great wind threshing the side of the hill. Amidst the din, the cries of the poor lepers were not more than the twittering of dazed sparrows.

The moment of the meeting of the hosts was come, and with it the opportunity the sufferers were seeking; if not taken, it would be lost forever, and they would be lost as well.

"Nearer, my child—let us get nearer. He cannot hear us," said the mother.

She arose, and staggered forward. Her ghastly hands were up, and she screamed with horrible shrillness. The people saw her—saw her hideous face, and stopped awe-struck—an effect for which extreme human misery, visible as in this instance, is as potent as majesty in purple and gold. Tirzah, behind her a little way, fell down too faint and frightened to follow farther.

"The lepers! the lepers!"

"Stone them!"

"The accursed of God! Kill them!"

These, with other yells of like import, broke in upon the hosannas of the part of the multitude too far removed to see and understand the cause of the interruption.

> Some there were, however, near by familiar with the nature of the man to whom the unfortunates were appealing—some who, by long intercourse with him, had caught somewhat of his divine compassion: they gazed at him, and were silent while, in fair view, he rode up and stopped in front of the woman. She also beheld his face—calm, pitiful, and of exceeding beauty, the large eyes tender with benignant purpose.
>
> And this was the colloquy that ensued:
>
> "O Master, Master! Thou seest our need; thou canst make us clean. Have mercy upon us—mercy!"
>
> "Believest thou I am able to do this?" he asked.
>
> "Thou art he of whom the prophets spake—thou art the Messiah!" she replied.
>
> His eyes grew radiant, his manner confident.
>
> "Woman," he said, "great is thy faith; be it unto thee even as thou wilt."
>
> He lingered an instant after, apparently unconscious of the presence of the throng—an instant—then he rode away.

You'll notice that, although he inserted his own characters into the scene, Wallace stuck to his policy of never putting any words in Christ's mouth that were not actually taken from the Gospels.

What did it feel like to be healed of leprosy by faith? Wallace imagines it as a feeling as much in the spirit as in the body:

> There was first in the hearts of the lepers a freshening of the blood; then it flowed faster and stronger, thrilling their wasted bodies with an infinitely sweet sense of painless healing. Each felt the scourge going from her; their

> strength revived; they were returning to be themselves. Directly, as if to make the purification complete, from body to spirit the quickening ran, exalting them to a very fervor of ecstasy. The power possessing them to this good end was most nearly that of a draught of swift and happy effect; yet it was unlike and superior in that its healing and cleansing were absolute, and not merely a delicious consciousness while in progress, but the planting, growing, and maturing all at once of a recollection so singular and so holy that the simple thought of it should be of itself ever after a formless yet perfect thanksgiving.[33]

How does a Christian react to this scene—or to any of the healings of leprosy we see in the Gospels? Yes, we think it's very nice that Jesus stopped to heal someone's leprosy. It's just the sort of thing we like about him. But if we take our faith seriously, we take Jesus as our model. If he treated people with leprosy as human beings, so must we. It isn't easy. It certainly wasn't easy when there still wasn't a cure for leprosy. Yet Christians did it—not all of them, to be sure, but enough of them to make it obvious that something new had entered the world.

When Christianity was made legal in the Roman Empire, Christians had an opportunity to institutionalize their care of the sick. St. Basil the Great, bishop of Caesarea in Cappadocia (a place in Asia Minor, not to be confused with any of the other Caesareas scattered throughout the empire), built a complex of hospital and charity home that grew so large that people started calling it the New City. At Basil's funeral, his friend Gregory of Nazianzus described it as one of the wonders of the world:

[33] *Ben-Hur*, bk. 8, chap. 4.

> Go forth a little way from the city, and behold the new city, the storehouse of piety, the common treasury of the wealthy, in which the superfluities of their wealth, aye, and even their necessaries, are stored, in consequence of his exhortations, freed from the power of the moth [Matt. 6:19], no longer gladdening the eyes of the thief, and escaping both the emulation of envy, and the corruption of time: where disease is regarded in a religious light, and disaster is thought a blessing, and sympathy is put to the test.
>
> Why should I compare with this work Thebes of the seen portals, and the Egyptian Thebes, and the walls of Babylon, and the Carian tomb of Mausolus, and the Pyramids, and the bronze without weight of the Colossus, or the size and beauty of shrines that are no more, and all the other objects of men's wonder, and historic record, from which their founders gained no advantage, except a slight meed of fame? My subject is the most wonderful of all, the short road to salvation, the easiest ascent to heaven.[34]

That list of things not to be compared with Basil's work includes several of the famous Seven Wonders of the World—the Mausoleum, the Colossus, the Pyramids. Basil's hospital is more wonderful than all of them, Gregory says. He goes on to describe exactly how the treatment of people with leprosy has changed because of Basil:

> There is no longer before our eyes that terrible and piteous spectacle of men who are living corpses, the greater part of whose limbs have mortified, driven away from their

[34] Gregory of Nazianzus, *Orations* 43.63, "On the Great St. Basil."

cities and homes and public places and fountains, aye, and from their own dearest ones, recognizable by their names rather than by their features: they are no longer brought before us at our gatherings and meetings, in our common intercourse and union, no longer the objects of hatred, instead of pity on account of their disease; composers of piteous songs, if any of them have their voice still left to them. Why should I try to express in tragic style all our experiences, when no language can be adequate to their hard lot?

He however it was, who took the lead in pressing upon those who were men, that they ought not to despise their fellow men, nor to dishonor Christ, the one Head of all, by their inhuman treatment of them; but to use the misfortunes of others as an opportunity of firmly establishing their own lot, and to lend to God that mercy of which they stand in need at His hands.

He did not therefore disdain to honor with his lips this disease, noble and of noble ancestry and brilliant reputation though he was, but saluted them as brethren, not, as some might suppose, from vanity (for who was so far removed from this feeling?), but taking the lead in approaching to tend them, as a consequence of his philosophy, and so giving not only a speaking, but also a silent, instruction.

The effect produced is to be seen not only in the city, but in the country and beyond, and even the leaders of society have vied with one another in their philanthropy and magnanimity towards them. Others have had their cooks, and splendid tables, and the devices and dainties of confectioners, and exquisite carriages, and soft, flowing

> robes; Basil's care was for the sick, and the relief of their wounds, and the imitation of Christ, by cleansing leprosy, not by a word, but in deed.

It would be hard to paint a clearer picture of the difference between the old and the new ways of confronting leprosy. Fear and hatred were the normal reactions to leprosy throughout the ancient world; but Basil taught his flock a better way. His hospital was founded on the idea that lepers are people whose disease is a misfortune, not a punishment they have deserved for some sin they committed.

It's even worth noting that Gregory has to defend his brother from charges of "vanity." Before the Christian revolution, how would that charge have made sense at all? Who would be *proud* of associating with lepers and treating them as brothers? The fear of leprosy had not been conquered—it still hasn't been conquered in our world today. But the idea that it's *good* to treat the victims of the disease as human beings had actually taken hold. Now the envious and lazy could mutter under their breaths that Basil was doing all this work for the sick just to make himself look good.

The Christians did not make distinctions in religion, either, when they were helping the sick. Julian the Apostate was a descendant of Constantine who, when he became emperor, tried to turn the empire back to paganism. It didn't work, of course. Even Julian's paganism wasn't the old paganism of Rome: it was thoroughly infected by Christian ideas. Much as he despised Christians, Julian had a Christian moral sense. He writes to his pagan priests in Galatia:

> I have ordered Galatia to supply you with thirty thousand bushels of wheat every year, of which the fifth part is to be given to the poor who attend on the priests, and the

> remainder to be distributed among strangers and our own beggars. For when none of the Jews beg, and the impious Galileans [Julian's would-be insulting name for Christians] relieve both their own poor and ours, it is shameful that ours should be destitute of our assistance.[35]

Even Julian is forced to acknowledge that, pagan or Christian, the poor of Galatia get their help from the Christians. You may also notice that the pagan priests are getting state funding to care for the poor, whereas the Christians were doing it with their own money.

Today, whatever our complaints about our health-care system, we take it for granted that sick people aren't chased out of town by mobs throwing rocks at them. Sickness is a misfortune, not a judgment, and the sick have our sympathy. The way people with leprosy are treated in *Ben-Hur* reminds us just how much of a revolution that attitude is.

[35] Julian, Epistle 49, to Arsacius, high priest of Galatia, in *Select Works of the Emperor Julian*, trans. by John Duncombe (London: T. Caddell, 1784), 129.

10

The Truth about the Gladiator Games

We come to the climax now. Judah challenges Messala—once his friend, now his mortal enemy—to a chariot race with everything at stake. Even their very lives.

We're appalled by the complete disregard for human life in the chariot-race scene in *Ben-Hur*, and we wonder whether it could really have been that bad. Then we learn more about what the Romans thought of as entertainment, and we realize that it was actually a great deal worse.

The chariot race made the reputation of the book, so of course it's the thing every movie version has to get right.

> And now, to make the turn, Messala began to draw in his left-hand steeds, an act which necessarily slackened their speed. His spirit was high; more than one altar was richer of his vows; the Roman genius was still president. On the three pillars only six hundred feet away were fame, increase of fortune, promotions, and a triumph ineffably sweetened by hate, all in store for him! That moment Malluch, in the gallery, saw Ben-Hur lean forward over his Arabs, and give them the reins. Out flew the many-folded lash in his hand; over the backs of the startled

steeds it writhed and hissed, and hissed and writhed again and again; and though it fell not, there were both sting and menace in its quick report; and as the man passed thus from quiet to resistless action, his face suffused, his eyes gleaming, along the reins he seemed to flash his will; and instantly not one, but the four as one, answered with a leap that landed them alongside the Roman's car. Messala, on the perilous edge of the goal, heard, but dared not look to see what the awakening portended. From the people he received no sign. Above the noises of the race there was but one voice, and that was Ben-Hur's. In the old Aramaic, as the sheik himself, he called to the Arabs:

"On, Atair! On, Rigel! What, Antares! dost thou linger now? Good horse—oho, Aldebaran! I hear them singing in the tents. I hear the children singing and the women—singing of the stars, of Atair, Antares, Rigel, Aldebaran, victory!—and the song will never end. Well done! Home to-morrow, under the black tent—home! On, Antares! The tribe is waiting for us, and the master is waiting! 'Tis done! 'tis done! Ha, ha! We have overthrown the proud. The hand that smote us is in the dust. Ours the glory! Ha, ha!—steady! The work is done—soho! Rest!"

There had never been anything of the kind more simple; seldom anything so instantaneous.

At the moment chosen for the dash, Messala was moving in a circle round the goal. To pass him, Ben-Hur had to cross the track, and good strategy required the movement to be in a forward direction; that is, on a like circle limited to the least possible increase. The thousands on the benches understood it all: they saw the signal given—the magnificent response; the four close outside Messala's outer wheel; Ben-Hur's inner wheel behind the other's car—all this they saw. Then they heard a crash loud enough to send a thrill through the Circus, and, quicker than thought, out over the course a spray of shining white and yellow flinders flew. Down on its right side toppled the bed of the Roman's chariot. There was a rebound as of the axle hitting the hard earth; another and another; then the car went to pieces; and Messala, entangled in the reins, pitched forward headlong.

To increase the horror of the sight by making death certain, the Sidonian, who had the wall next behind, could not stop or turn out. Into the wreck full speed he drove; then over the Roman, and into the latter's four, all mad with fear. Presently, out of the turmoil, the fighting of horses, the resound of blows, the murky cloud of dust and sand, he crawled, in time to see the Corinthian and Byzantine go on down the course after Ben-Hur, who had not been an instant delayed.

The people arose, and leaped upon the benches, and shouted and screamed. Those who looked that way caught glimpses of Messala, now under the trampling of the fours, now under the abandoned cars. He was still; they thought him dead; but far the greater number followed Ben-Hur in his career. They had not seen the cunning touch of the reins by which, turning a little to the left, he caught Messala's wheel with the iron-shod point of his axle, and crushed it; but they had seen the transformation of the man, and themselves felt the heat and glow of his spirit, the heroic resolution, the maddening energy of action with which, by look, word, and gesture, he so suddenly

> inspired his Arabs. And such running! It was rather the long leaping of lions in harness; but for the lumbering chariot, it seemed the four were flying. When the Byzantine and Corinthian were halfway down the course, Ben-Hur turned the first goal.
>
> And the race was won!
>
> The consul arose; the people shouted themselves hoarse; the editor came down from his seat, and crowned the victors.[36]

The Roman games were much like our big-league sports in many ways: they drew tens of thousands of people, they produced celebrity players whose names everyone recognized, and they formed the main subject of conversation for days afterward. But they were also different in very important ways. They were not just games: they were religious ceremonies.

There were dozens of holidays in the Roman calendar—probably about seventy-five by the time of our hero Judah Ben-Hur.[37] Even in English, the word *holiday* comes from *holy day*—a day of some religious observance. With all the gods and goddesses in the Roman pantheon, there were plenty of occasions for religious observances.

A holiday wasn't just a day off work. It was a day when certain rites were celebrated to please the gods or commemorate some important event in history.

The games started as religious rites, paid for by the government, and administered by the officials the people had elected to take care of them. After speculating a little on the etymology

[36] *Ben-Hur*, bk. 5, chap. 14.

[37] Richard C. Beacham, *Spectacle Entertainments of Ancient Rome* (New Haven: Yale University Press, 1999), 2.

of the names of the various games, the Christian writer Tertullian goes on to explain the real reason a Christian can't have anything to do with them: they're all pagan religious rites.

> However, it is of little consequence the origin of the name, when it is certain that the thing springs from idolatry.
>
> The Liberalia, under the general designation of "games," clearly declared the glory of Father Bacchus; for to Bacchus these festivities were first consecrated by grateful peasants, in return for the boon he conferred on them, as they say, making known the pleasures of wine.
>
> Then the Consualia were called "games," and at first were in honor of Neptune, for Neptune has the name of Consus also. Thereafter Romulus dedicated the Equiria to Mars. But then they claim the Consualia too for Romulus, on the ground that he consecrated them to Consus, the god, as they will have it, of counsel. In fact it was the *counsel* by which he planned the rape of the Sabine virgins as wives for his soldiers. Oh, yes, that's a fine piece of *counsel*, and I suppose it's still considered quite just and righteous by the Romans themselves, though not necessarily by God.[38]

Tertullian—in case you couldn't guess—was known for his sarcasm, which he never spared when he was riled up about something.

He goes on to remind his readers that it's not just the games of long ago. All the games in his own supposedly enlightened and civilized age have pagan names to go with their pagan origins.

[38] Tertullian, *De Spectaculis* 5, in Alexander Roberts and James Donaldson, eds., *Ante-Nicene Christian Library* (New York: Christian Literature Publishing Company, 1885), vol. 9, 13-14.

> To the testimony of antiquity is added that of later games instituted in their turn, and betraying their origin from the titles which they bear even at the present day, in which it is imprinted as on their very face for what idol and for what religious object games, whether of the one kind or the other, were designed. You have festivals bearing the name of the great Mother and Apollo, of Ceres too, and Neptune, and Jupiter Latiaris, and Flora, all celebrated for a common end; the others have their religious origin in the birthdays and solemnities of kings, in public successes, in municipal holidays. There are also testamentary exhibitions, in which funeral honours are rendered to the memories of private persons; and this according to an institution of ancient times. For from the first the games were regarded as of two sorts, sacred and funereal—that is, in honour of the heathen deities and of the dead.[39]

According to modern scholars, Tertullian gets the origin of the games right. Every one of them began as some sort of religious or funerary celebration. Gladiatorial combats, for example, were usual at funerals of important men. The bigger the gladiatorial show, the more important the deceased obviously was, and therefore the more important his surviving son who arranged for the games was.

But a funny thing happened to those games.

Remember that, until a little before the birth of Christ, Rome was a republic. The Rome that conquered the world was a city

[39] Tertullian, *De Spectaculis* 6, in Roberts and Donaldson, *Ante-Nicene Christian Library*, vol. 9, 14-15.

run by elected officials. After the empire began, the elected officials still held their positions—it was just that there was an emperor at the top of the heap who could tell them what to do. There were still elections to win, and winning them brought honor, status, and wealth to the winners, even if it had little effect on the ultimate course of government.

A Roman politician, like any politician, was always looking toward the next position. His term of office would expire soon—most offices lasted only a year—and then he would have to run for another office. The law said he couldn't have the same office two years in a row. Of course he hoped to move up to a better, more honorable, more remunerative position.

The Romans had a word for this upward progression: the *cursus honorum*—course of offices. There was a particular order in which an ambitious politician would move through the various offices: quaestor, aedile, praetor, consul. You couldn't repeat the same office, so you had to move forward and upward. Each office had a minimum age requirement, and the politician who managed to win each office at the youngest possible age was very proud of himself. The famous orator Cicero was consul at the youngest possible age, for example, and lost no opportunity to crow about it.

There was one obvious good thing about the system. It was a strong encouragement for the ambitious politician to please the people: if they liked his performance in this office, they would elect him to the next one right away. On the other hand, it was also a strong encouragement for the politician to think *only* of pleasing the people. His next position depended not on how well or how justly he had exercised his power, but on how happy he made the voters.

That problem comes up with every elected government, of course. But in the Roman government, it had a strong effect on the games in particular. In an age with no television, no private theaters, no other forms of entertainment, the games were the things ordinary people really looked forward to. Rome had grown rapidly into the largest city on earth: it was crowded, dirty, and hectic. For the average Roman, it was always the same. Except on the holidays.

Chariot races, stage plays, gladiator fights—they might all be part of the sacred games. And the more spectacular the show, the more the people liked it. The more the people liked it, the better they liked the aedile who was responsible for the show. And the more they liked that aedile this year, the more likely he was to be a praetor next year.

There was a limited budget for the games. But there was no law against the aedile's spending his own money to supplement the official budget. An aedile could make the show just a bit more exciting, just a bit more spectacular, with just a bit more money. And that gave him just a bit of advantage in the next election.

If you know anything about politics, you know how that went. More money made more of a spectacle, and that made more of a difference in the popularity of the official who put it on. And more money than that made more difference than that. Just as our politicians of today seem to be caught in a never-ending race to outspend each other on election campaigns, so the Roman politicians were in a never-ending race to outspend each other on the games.

Gladiatorial games had originally been for funerals. But politicians whose fathers died started delaying the games until the end of the year—election season. The connection between the games and the ambition of the politician who gave them was made completely obvious when Julius Caesar staged the most enormous gladiatorial show Rome had ever seen in honor of his father—who had died twenty years earlier. (But Caesar was still sad about it.)

The politician and famous orator Cicero thought the extravagance was shameful. Not the business of killing people for entertainment purposes, mind you, but the extravagance of spending all that money on it. A Roman might well say that gladiatorial battles were a *good* moral influence: they hardened the population to the kind of martial exercise that made victorious soldiers. But the extravagance! Think of all the better ways that money could be spent.

Nevertheless, Cicero knew that even the best and most honest politicians had to give the people the shows they craved.

> I know very well that it has been an ancient custom in this city, even in virtuous times, to expect show and splendor even from the best men in the time of their aedileship. P. Crassus the Rich (as well in his fortune as in his name) in his office of aedile, entertained the people with a show of prodigious expense; then L. Crassus, sometime after him, held the same office with great magnificence, though joined with Q. Mucius too, a man of singular moderation. And then C. Claudius, the son of Appius, with a great many more; as the two Luculli, Hortensius, Silanus, which were all outdone by P. Lentulus in my consulship: and Scaurus emulated him. But the most pompous and expensive solemnity of all was that of our friend Pompey in his second consulship. This is enough to show you my opinion in all these cases.
>
> No man however should be so far moderate, as to draw upon himself the suspicion of avarice. Mamercus, a

> person of very great riches, was put by the consulship for no other reason, but because he refused to be aedile first.

So you don't want to spend *too* much money on the games, because that would be—well, vulgar. But, on the other hand, you can't afford to be seen as a cheapskate.

> If such things therefore are demanded by the people, and allowed of, though perhaps not *desired*, by good men, then they must be performed; but so as to keep within the compass of your estate, as I myself did. Nay, though they should not be *demanded* by the people, yet they might wisely enough be presented them, upon a prospect of gaining some more considerable advantage by it....
>
> But the best way of laying out money in this kind is to repair the city walls, make docks, havens, aqueducts, and the like—things that may serve to the general use and advantage of the public.[40]

Yes, Cicero thinks useful public works are the best way to spend money—and wealthy ambitious politicians sometimes did that, too, giving the public grand buildings and aqueducts that would carry the name of the donor into history. Still, even Cicero has to admit that, when it comes right down to it, you're probably going to have to give the people some shows. He sounds like a current politician justifying taking PAC money for his campaign: yes, it leaves a bad taste in your mouth, but you have to do it to get elected—and you can't do any good for the people if you don't get elected, can you?

[40] Cicero, *Offices*, adapted from the translation by Sir Ralph L'Estrange (London: D. Browne, R. Knaplock, B. Tooke, G. Strahan, J. Tonson, S. Ballard, W. Mears, and F. Clay, 1720), 134-136.

The same forces that bloated the games into the huge spectacles the people of Rome came to expect were at work in the provinces. A big city such as Antioch would have games to rival Rome's; a small provincial town might have a small provincial show, but it would be the biggest show that town's officials could afford.

Tertullian regards them all as equally bad, the big-city spectacles and the small-town shows, because they were all ultimately pagan religious celebrations. He describes very vividly the grand parade that came before the show—a parade that functioned the same way a circus parade functions today: it advertised the show to come and got people into a celebratory mood. But it was always a religious procession, not just a big show:

> But the more ambitious preliminary display of the circus games, to which the name "procession" belongs in particular, proves in itself what the whole thing is about, in the many images, the long line of statues, the chariots of all sorts, the thrones, the crowns, the dresses. And what high religious rites besides! What sacrifices before, during, and after! How many guilds, how many priesthoods, how many offices are set astir! You know all about it if you live in the great city in which the demon convention has its headquarters.
>
> If these things are done in humbler style in the provinces just because there's not as much money to pay for them, still all circus games must be counted as belonging to that from which they are derived. The fountain from which they spring defiles them. For the tiny streamlet from its very spring-head, the little twig from its very budding, contains in it the essential nature of its origin. It may be

> grand or mean—no matter: any circus procession whatever is offensive to God. Even if there are not very many images to grace it, there is idolatry in one. Even if there is no more than a single sacred car, it is a chariot of Jupiter. Anything of idolatry whatever, whether meanly arrayed or modestly rich and gorgeous, taints it in its origin.[41]

The parade was good for getting people into a celebratory mood. But it wasn't what the people were there for. They had come to be entertained. And what entertained them was death.

Charioteers risked death in their rickety chariots, made as light as possible to be as fast as possible. Gladiators risked death in every fight. But at least charioteers and gladiators had some chance of surviving through their skill. There was another class of games, often added to the gladiator shows, in which condemned prisoners "fought" wild animals. The animals—lions, leopards, wild boars, and every other kind of dangerous creature—were chosen to be as vicious as possible. The condemned prisoners were unarmed: their only job was to die in the bloodiest way possible, so that the audience could enjoy themselves. As the illegal Christian cult grew, Roman magistrates often found victims for the beasts among the Christians.

It happens that we have a very complete description of some of these "games," because Christians preserved the memories of their martyrs very carefully. One group of martyrs included Perpetua and Felicity, two women condemned for their faith to be mauled by the beasts. Felicity had just given birth to a child, which earned her no sympathy at all. The Christian writer tells

[41] Tertullian, *De Spectaculis* 7, in Roberts and Donaldson, *Ante-Nicene Christian Library*, vol. 9, 15.

us exactly how much the audience enjoyed the spectacle of a young mother being torn to shreds.

> The day of their victory shone forth, and they proceeded from the prison into the amphitheatre, as if to an assembly, joyous and of brilliant countenance; if perchance shrinking, it was with joy, and not with fear. Perpetua followed with placid look, and with step and gait as a matron of Christ, beloved of God; casting down the luster of her eyes from the gaze of all. Moreover, Felicity, rejoicing that she had safely brought forth, so that she might fight with the wild beasts; from the blood and from the midwife to the gladiator, to wash after childbirth with a second baptism.
>
> And when they were brought to the gate, and were constrained to put on the clothing—the men, that of the priests of Saturn, and the women, that of those who were consecrated to Ceres—that noble-minded woman resisted even to the end with constancy. For she said, "We have come thus far of our own accord, for this reason, that our liberty might not be restrained. For this reason we have yielded our minds, that we might not do any such thing as this: we have agreed on this with you."

It is hard for us today to understand the notion of "religion" represented here, but it's a vital part of the "games."

Remember what the audience came here to see: wild animals goaded into killing unarmed men and women, including a mother who has just given birth. And they will cheer for the animals. There will be a variety of animals, so that there can be a variety of styles of killing. It would be boring if all the victims were ripped apart in exactly the same way.

But somehow this is a *religious* celebration. It is pleasing to the gods. The male victims will be dressed as priests of Saturn, and the females as priestesses of Ceres. We might think this was the height of blasphemy, a crudely obscene joke that shows utter contempt for the cults of Ceres and Saturn. But it's exactly the reverse: although the games are an extravagant entertainment for a jaded population, their fundamental purpose is religious. These people are gathered to *honor* Ceres and Saturn by watching leopards and boars rip human beings to shreds.

Here is where Felicity, the prisoner and intended victim who really should have no power at all, shows a strength of conviction that seems to surprise her captors. She will not wear the pagan robes. She will go willingly to be torn to shreds by animals, but she will not do it in the uniform of a priestess of Ceres.

> Injustice acknowledged the justice; the tribune yielded to their being brought as simply as they were. Perpetua sang psalms, already treading under foot the head of the Egyptian; Revocatus, and Saturninus, and Saturus uttered threatenings against the gazing people about this martyrdom. When they came within sight of Hilarianus, by gesture and nod, they began to say to Hilarianus, "You judge us," they said, "but God will judge you."

The translator has filled out the terse original a bit here. The martyrs could not be heard in the huge stadium over the roar of the crowd; they communicated by gesture alone, and it was probably a gesture they had coordinated in advance. They pointed to the judge Hilarianus, and then to themselves; then they pointed to heaven, and then to Hilarianus.

The meaning was absolutely clear, and the crowd definitely got it.

> At this the people, exasperated, demanded that they should be tormented with scourges as they passed along the rank of the venatores [the professional beast wranglers]. And they indeed rejoiced that they should have incurred any one of their Lord's passions.
>
> But He who had said, "Ask, and ye shall receive," gave to them when they asked, that death which each one had wished for. For when at any time they had been discoursing among themselves about their wish in respect of their martyrdom, Saturninus indeed had professed that he wished that he might be thrown to all the beasts; doubtless that he might wear a more glorious crown. Therefore in the beginning of the exhibition, he and Revocatus made trial of the leopard, and moreover upon the scaffold they were harassed by the bear. Saturus, however, held nothing in greater abomination than a bear; but he imagined that he would be put an end to with one bite of a leopard. Therefore, when a wild boar was supplied, it was the huntsman rather who had supplied that boar who was gored by that same beast, and died the day after the shows. Saturus only was drawn out; and when he had been bound on the floor near to a bear, the bear would not come forth from his den. And so Saturus for the second time was recalled unhurt.
>
> Moreover, for the young women the devil prepared a very fierce cow, provided especially for that purpose contrary to custom, rivaling their sex also in that of the beasts. And so, stripped and clothed with nets, they were

led forth. The populace shuddered as they saw one young woman of delicate frame, and another with breasts still drooping from her recent childbirth. So, being recalled, they are unbound. Perpetua is first led in. She was tossed, and fell on her loins; and when she saw her tunic torn from her side, she drew it over her as a veil for her middle, rather mindful of her modesty than her suffering.

Then she was called for again, and bound up her dishevelled hair; for it was not becoming for a martyr to suffer with dishevelled hair, lest she should appear to be mourning in her glory. So she rose up; and when she saw Felicitas crushed, she approached and gave her her hand, and lifted her up. And both of them stood together; and the brutality of the populace being appeased, they were recalled to the Sanavivarian gate. Then Perpetua was received by a certain one who was still a catechumen, Rusticus by name, who kept close to her; and she, as if aroused from sleep, so deeply had she been in the Spirit and in an ecstasy, began to look round her, and to say to the amazement of all, "I cannot tell when we are to be led out to that cow." And when she had heard what had already happened, she did not believe it until she had perceived certain signs of injury in her body and in her dress, and had recognized the catechumen. Afterwards causing that catechumen and the brother to approach, she addressed them, saying, "Stand fast in the faith, and love one another, all of you, and be not offended at my sufferings."

The same Saturus at the other entrance exhorted the soldier Pudens, saying, "Assuredly here I am, as I have promised and foretold, for up to this moment I have felt no beast. And now believe with your whole heart. Lo, I am going forth to that beast, and I shall be destroyed with one bite of the leopard."

And immediately at the conclusion of the exhibition he was thrown to the leopard; and with one bite of his he was bathed with such a quantity of blood, that the people shouted out to him as he was returning, the testimony of his second baptism, "Saved and washed, saved and washed." Manifestly he was assuredly saved who had been glorified in such a spectacle.

Then to the soldier Pudens he said, "Farewell, and be mindful of my faith; and let not these things disturb, but confirm you." And at the same time he asked for a little ring from his finger, and returned it to him bathed in his wound, leaving to him an inherited token and the memory of his blood. And then lifeless he is cast down with the rest, to be slaughtered in the usual place.

And when the populace called for them into the midst, that as the sword penetrated into their body they might make their eyes partners in the murder, they rose up of their own accord, and transferred themselves whither the people wished; but they first kissed one another, that they might consummate their martyrdom with the kiss of peace. The rest indeed, immoveable and in silence, received the sword-thrust; much more Saturus, who also had first ascended the ladder, and first gave up his spirit, for he also was waiting for Perpetua.

But Perpetua, that she might taste some pain, being pierced between the ribs, cried out loudly, and she herself placed the wavering right hand of the youthful gladiator to her throat. Possibly such a woman could not have

> been slain unless she herself had willed it, because she was feared by the impure spirit.[42]

Now, reading this description, we can see that any former moral justification the games might have had, from the most generous point of view, is simply gone. If we thought preparation for war was the highest virtue in a citizen, then we could have said of the early gladiator shows that they put the virtues we wanted from our soldiers on display. But here we just have leopards killing people, and the gladiator's victim is an unarmed woman. It's pure sadism, nothing more. And the crowd goes wild.

These martyrdoms in the arena became part of the enduring legacy of early Christianity—stories the Christians told each other for centuries afterward. We're still telling them today.

So it's shocking to discover that the games did not stop when Christianity became the religion of the empire. Christians were no longer being mauled by leopards, but there were still gladiator fights in the big cities. Why were they not banned? Well, they were. Constantine, the first Christian emperor, banned gladiator fights in 325. Prisoners who had been condemned to fight in the arena would be sent to work in the mines instead.

Suppressing the games was clearly the Christian thing to do. But the suppression didn't last long. We know that Constantine himself gave games a few years after his own edict, so apparently it was harder than he thought to ban the gladiators.

Yet Christian leaders had always been loud in their condemnations of the games. Decades before Constantine, when Christianity was still an illegal cult, St. Cyprian of Carthage condemned

42 *The Passion of Perpetua and Felicitas*, in Alexander Roberts and James Donaldson, eds., *The Ante-Nicene Fathers*, vol. 3 (New York: Charles Scribner's Sons, 1903), 704-705.

the gladiatorial shows in the most vigorous terms. He was speaking, as you'll see, of the shows in which the gladiators were *voluntary*, not the ones in which Christians were thrown to beasts—a different subject altogether.

> Just for a moment, imagine that you have been transported to one of the loftiest peaks of some inaccessible mountain. From there, gaze on the appearances of things lying below you, and with eyes turned in various directions look upon the eddies of the billowy world, while you yourself are removed from earthly contacts. You will at once begin to feel compassion for the world, and with self-recollection and increasing gratitude to God, you will rejoice with all the greater joy that you have escaped it....
>
> And now, if you turn your eyes and your regards to the cities themselves, you will behold a concourse more fraught with sadness than any solitude. The gladiatorial games are prepared, that blood may gladden the lust of cruel eyes. The body is fed up with stronger food, and the vigorous mass of limbs is enriched with brawn and muscle, that the wretch fattened for punishment may die a harder death. Man is slaughtered that man may be gratified, and the skill that is best able to kill is an exercise and an art. Crime is not only committed, but it is taught. What can be said more inhuman—what more repulsive? Training is undergone to acquire the power to murder, and the achievement of murder is its glory.
>
> What state of things, I pray you, can that be, and what can it be like, in which men, whom none have condemned, offer themselves to the wild beasts—men of ripe age, of sufficiently beautiful person, clad in costly

> garments? Living men, they are adorned for a voluntary death; wretched men, they boast of their own miseries. They fight with beasts, not for their crime, but for their madness. Fathers look on their own sons; a brother is in the arena, and his sister is hard by; and although a grander display of pomp increases the price of the exhibition, yet, oh shame! even the mother will pay the increase in order that she may be present at her own miseries. And in looking upon scenes so frightful and so impious and so deadly, they do not seem to be aware that they are parricides with their eyes.[43]

So we've seen Tertullian condemning the games because they all are pagan religious ceremonies, and therefore a Christian can have nothing to do with them. We have seen that the Christians associated the arenas with martyrdom. And we have seen Cyprian condemning the games because they are cruel and murderous—accusations that would have struck an earlier pagan as nonsensical, but that make perfect sense to us, with our Christian worldview.

So why were the games not suppressed, even when Constantine tried to suppress them?

We learn the reason from the story of the later suppression of the games by the emperor Honorius in 399. The church historian Theodoret gives us a brief report:

> Honorius, who inherited the empire of Europe, put a stop to the gladiatorial combats which had long been held at

[43] Cyprian, Epistle I to Donatus, adapted from the translation by the Rev. Robert Ernest Wallis, *Writings of Cyprian* (Edinburgh: T. and T. Clark, 1868), 6.

> Rome. The occasion of his doing so arose from the following circumstance. A certain man of the name of Telemachus had embraced the ascetic life. He had set out from the East and for this reason had repaired to Rome. There, when the abominable spectacle was being exhibited, he went himself into the stadium, and, stepping down into the arena, endeavored to stop the men who were wielding their weapons against one another. The spectators of the slaughter were indignant, and inspired by the mad fury of the demon who delights in those bloody deeds, stoned the peacemaker to death.
>
> When the admirable emperor was informed of this he numbered Telemachus in the army of victorious martyrs, and put an end to that impious spectacle.[44]

There's the answer to why the games hadn't been suppressed yet: because if you tried to suppress them, the spectators would kill you. In modern terms, think of it this way: imagine a university president at a popular football school saying, "We're going to close down the football program because the injuries to young athletes, for whom we have a duty of care, are unacceptable." Ask yourself how long that person would remain a university president.

You will not often hear Honorius called "admirable" by historians who were not directly in the pay of Honorius, but he did ban the gladiator shows in the year 399. The Christian historian gives him credit for that, and rightly so. Honorius also banned

[44] Theodoret, *Ecclesiastical History*, bk. 5, chap. 26, in Philip Schaff and Henry Wace, eds., *Nicene and Post-Nicene Fathers*, second series (New York: Christian Literature Company, 1892), vol. 3, 151.

the gladiator shows in 404. Valentinian III banned them in 438. It took a lot of banning to get rid of the games. Christian emperors kept trying, because the gladiator fights were obviously against every Christian principle; but the people wanted their games. And the city of Rome—whose upper class clung to paganism long after it had died out in most other cities—was no longer the residence of the emperors, who in the Western empire usually made their capital at Milan or Ravenna by this time. Pagan city aristocrats could continue to give games that the emperor would probably never hear about, or that he would shrug off if he did hear about them. It was more than a century before the gladiator shows were actually suppressed in Rome.

What was this madness that came over people, so that they would all gang together and kill a monk rather than let him interrupt the fight? We've heard news stories about sports-related violence in our own world, from the celebratory couch-burnings after college games to the "football hooliganism" that sometimes ends in massacre. The psychology is probably very similar. In fact, we have a psychological portrait of one sports fan of the late 300s, because St. Augustine had a good friend named Alipius, who became addicted to the gladiatorial "games" in spite of his strong moral prejudice against them. It's a fascinating story: every other description of the games concentrates on what went on in the arena, but Augustine concentrates on what went on in the minds of the spectators.

As it so often does with young men, the problem began with peer pressure.

> Not forsaking the way of this world, which his parents inculcated to him, Alipius had gone to Rome before me to study the law; and there was again carried away with

an incredible passion to the shows of the gladiators, and after an incredible manner.

Even though he was very much averse from, and detested these sports, some of his friends and schoolfellows meeting him in the streets after dinner, with a friendly violence led him along with them much against his will to the amphitheater on a day when those cruel and tragic sports were exhibited. He was resisting all the while, and telling them, "If you drag my body there along with you, and place it there, can you force me to turn my mind or my eyes on those shows? Though present in body, I shall be absent, and so overcome both you and them."

Hearing this, they did not desist from drawing him along with them, having a mind perhaps to try whether he had power to do as he said.

When they got to the amphitheater, and had taken such places as they could, presently those cruel sports began.

But Alipius shutting the door of his eyes, forbid his soul to go out after such wicked objects. And would to God he had shut his ears too!

Some sort of accident happened in the fight. Hearing a great shout of all the people, he was overcome by curiosity, and opened his eyes, designing only to see what was the matter, and whatever it was, to despise it and overcome it. And he was immediately struck with a more grievous wound in the soul, than the gladiator, whom he desired to behold, was in the body, and he fell himself in a far more deplorable manner, than he at whose fall this shout was raised, which entering in at his ears had opened his eyes, and through them had given a mortal wound to his

> soul—which was more bold than strong, and indeed so much the weaker, because he presumed of himself, who should have confided only in you [God]. For no sooner did he see that blood, but he also drank down the savage cruelty of it; nor did he turn away his eyes, but fixed them upon it. And he sucked in those furies, and knew it not, and became delighted with the crime of the combat, and was madly drunk with that cruel pleasure. And he was not now the man that he came, but one of the multitude to which he came, and a true companion of those who brought him there.
>
> What more can I say? He looked on, he shouted, he took fire, he carried away with him a madness, by which he was incited to return again, not only with them who had dragged him thither before, but before them, and drawing others with him.
>
> And yet from hence also with your most strong and merciful hand you delivered him, and taught him to presume no more of himself, but to trust in you. But this was long afterwards.[45]

Augustine tells us elsewhere that this same friend of his was obsessed with the Carthaginian sports when he was in Carthage. They were not on the same scale as the ones in Rome, perhaps, but Carthage was a big city—the metropolis of the province of Africa. It would have had big, expensive shows.

You'll notice that Augustine has the typical Christian reaction. The shows are "crimes," "cruel pleasures," "a mortal wound

[45] Augustine, *Confessions*, bk. 6, chap. 8, adapted from the translation by Richard Challoner (Dublin: Farrell Kiernan, 1770).

to the soul." People who took their Christianity seriously kept up a constant pressure to end the spectacle of people killing each other for entertainment. The monk Telemachus even died to make his point. But the people wanted their shows.

We shake our heads today, but are we much better than the Romans?

Think of boxing. Yes, we don't expect to see a man killed in the boxing ring—not right away. But boxers all too frequently are gibbering idiots by middle age, done in by brain damage from so many blows to the head. Yet boxing is a sport carried on national television to be watched by tens of millions.

The same is true of football. We know that sixty-seven thousand high-school football players will be diagnosed with concussions every year, not counting many more that probably go undiagnosed.[46] How far would you get if you tried to ban football in your local high school?

Or think of auto racing. Is it really fun for the average spectator to watch cars go around and around in a circle? Or is the average spectator hoping for a fiery wreck to break up the monotony? On average, about one driver a year dies in a racing accident just in NASCAR, leaving aside all other kinds of racing.

So we ask ourselves: are we really so much better than the Romans? And the answer has to be yes.

[46] Thomas Talavage, Eric A. Nauman, Evan L. Breedlove, Umit Yoruk, Anne E. Dye, Katie Morigaki, Henry Feuer, and Larry J. Leverenz, "Functionally Detected Cognitive Impairment in High School Football Players without Clinically Diagnosed Concussion," *Journal of Neurotrauma* 31, no. 4 (2013): 327–338, archived on PubMed Central, retrieved August 2, 2015, https://www.ncbi.nlm.nih.gov/pmc/.

We play dangerous sports, but the Romans had "games" that were designed to be murder. We are imperfect at protecting our athletes; the Romans were disappointed if an unarmed mother failed to be mauled by the animals.

And we should not forget that we judge both the Romans and ourselves by Christian principles. It was Roman paganism that *invented* murder as entertainment. If paganism were to judge our sports today, it would have three words for us: *not enough blood*.

An interesting coda to our story: of all the Roman shows, the only one that survived far into the Christian era was the chariot races. In fact, they grew to be an obsession beyond what the Romans of Judah Ben-Hur's time could possibly have imagined. In Constantinople, the new imperial capital, the Red, White, Blue and Green teams were not just chariot-racing clubs: they were political parties. In a world in which the emperor was absolute, and there was no avenue for real participation in decision making, politics itself was almost treason. Thus, it found other ways to express itself, and the racetrack was the main avenue for that expression. Racing-based riots broke out year after year and, in the time of Justinian, destroyed a good part of the city.

But there were no more gladiators. Christianity finally won that battle.

11

What Became of Judah Ben-Hur?

Judah Ben-Hur has won the chariot race. Judah and Messala are reconciled. Judah's mother and sister are cured of their leprosy by a miracle. All their lives have been changed forever by the encounter with Christ.

Now what?

As a Jew, Judah Ben-Hur would have faced a choice: is Christ the Messiah, or isn't he?

Everything depends on that choice.

Let's imagine for the moment that Judah Ben-Hur is a real person of the first century. He has lived through the time when Christ was alive in Galilee and Judea. He has experienced one of the healing miracles of Christ—his own mother and sister cured of their leprosy. He has seen the Crucifixion and the mighty earthquake afterward.

But has he seen the Resurrection?

When Christ rose from the dead, he didn't appear all at once to the people of the whole world. But he didn't keep his Resurrection a secret, either. We know that he appeared to literally hundreds of people. Paul told the Corinthians:

> For I delivered to you as of first importance what I also received, that Christ died for our sins in accordance with the scriptures, that he was buried, that he was raised on the third day in accordance with the scriptures, and that he appeared to Cephas, then to the twelve. Then he appeared to more than five hundred brethren at one time, most of whom are still alive, though some have fallen asleep. Then he appeared to James, then to all the apostles. Last of all, as to one untimely born, he appeared also to me. (1 Cor. 15:3-8)

From the way he writes, it's obvious that he's reminding them of facts they already know. And they can check his facts: most of the people who saw the resurrected Christ, he says, are still alive. Hundreds of them. Just ask one of them.

Would Judah Ben-Hur have been one of those five hundred?

With the experiences he had had—standing at the foot of the Cross, seeing his mother and sister healed of leprosy, even finding the grace in his own heart to forgive Messala—we can hardly imagine that he wouldn't have been one of the followers of the Christ.

So what did that mean?

At first, it meant very little different from before, at least externally. Christ's followers had no separate name for their group. If they had to explain what was different about them, they said they were followers of the Way of salvation. But the Jewish followers of Christ lived like other Jews. They continued to go to the synagogue, or to the Temple if they were in Jerusalem.

But it was not easy for people who believed Jesus had been a criminal who deserved his execution to get along with people who believed he was the Son of God. A man named Stephen, one of the first group of helpers, or deacons, chosen to assist the apostles in dealing with the rapidly increasing numbers of converts, made quite an impression with his preaching—so much of an impression that members of several synagogues denounced him to the authorities.

When Stephen was brought before the council, he made the chief priests so angry with his defense that they hauled him out of the city and stoned him to death.

They were not angry enough, however, that they forgot to take off their expensive cloaks first. Wouldn't want to ruin those. They checked their cloaks with a man named Saul, who took good care of them while he watched approvingly as Stephen was murdered.

After that, the authorities decided they had had enough of these people. "And on that day," Luke tells us, "a great persecution arose against the church in Jerusalem; and they were all scattered throughout the region of Judea and Samaria, except the apostles. Devout men buried Stephen, and made great lamentation over him. But Saul was ravaging the church, and entering house after house, he dragged off men and women and committed them to prison" (Acts 8:1-3).

We can imagine that perhaps Judah Ben-Hur was among the scattered refugees. Or perhaps his family connection and his wealth would have been enough to keep him secure. But either way, these would have been difficult times for him if he was still in Jerusalem.

This persecution turned out to be a very bad strategic mistake. Yes, it frightened the believers and scattered them from Jerusalem. But now suddenly the Christian infection, which had been mostly confined to Jerusalem, was spreading all up and down the countryside. "Now those who were scattered went about preaching the word," Luke says (Acts 8:4). Everywhere those refugees went, they made converts to the Way.

Meanwhile, another very surprising thing happened. In the middle of a persecuting junket to Damascus, that Saul fellow who was so keen on ravaging the Church fell down on the road and got up a Christian. We know him now by his Greek name Paul, and he would turn into the most effective evangelist the Church has ever had.

It was not long, though, before differences of opinion came up among the followers of the Way. The main difference was about the Gentiles. Did they have to become fully Jewish to follow Christ?

That was a heavy burden. Not only were there the dietary restrictions and the innumerable other provisions of the Law—made more innumerable as time went on by the commentaries of the Pharisees—but there was also the matter of circumcision for the men. In a time of no anesthetics and no disinfectants, it was a painful and dangerous operation for an adult male. That would probably have been a deal-breaker for many of the converts right there.

We remember Peter's visit to Cornelius, when he had a vision telling him that all foods were made clean. Afterward, Peter had to explain himself to the people Luke calls "the circumcision party":

> So when Peter went up to Jerusalem, the circumcision party criticized him, saying, "Why did you go to uncircumcised men and eat with them?"
>
> But Peter began and explained to them in order: "I was in the city of Joppa praying; and in a trance I saw a vision,

> something descending, like a great sheet, let down from heaven by four corners; and it came down to me. Looking at it closely I observed animals and beasts of prey and reptiles and birds of the air. And I heard a voice saying to me, 'Rise, Peter; kill and eat.' But I said, 'No, Lord; for nothing common or unclean has ever entered my mouth.' But the voice answered a second time from heaven, 'What God has cleansed you must not call common.'" (Acts 11:2-9)

In this case, Luke tells us, Peter was persuasive:

> When they heard this they were silenced. And they glorified God, saying, "Then to the Gentiles also God has granted repentance unto life." (Acts 11:18)

But we know that the circumcision party persisted. Peter might have persuaded that one group, but there were others who were relentless in their opposition to the idea that the *uncircumcised* could be saved without overcoming the handicap of uncircumcision. They were so relentless, in fact, that they started to sway Peter, who—we remember from the Gospels—was exceptionally prone to swaying. Paul, who had been preaching to the Gentiles, was furious—and, characteristically, he told Peter exactly how furious he was, as he remembered later in a letter he wrote to the Christians in Galatia. The mere fact that Peter was Christ's chosen successor was not going to make Paul shut his mouth when he was sure that Peter was wrong.

> But when Cephas [Peter's Aramaic name] came to Antioch I opposed him to his face, because he stood condemned. For before certain men came from James, he ate with the Gentiles; but when they came he drew back and separated himself, fearing the circumcision party.

> And with him the rest of the Jews acted insincerely, so that even Barnabas was carried away by their insincerity. But when I saw that they were not straightforward about the truth of the gospel, I said to Cephas before them all, "If you, though a Jew, live like a Gentile and not like a Jew, how can you compel the Gentiles to live like Jews?" (Gal. 2:11-14)

Paul, too, uses that term "circumcision party," which Luke probably picked up from him. And you will notice that Paul confronted Peter "before them all." Paul was not the sort to take Peter aside gently and speak to him in low, respectful tones. It must have been a very embarrassing scene.

Here was another decision Judah Ben-Hur had to make. Assuming he followed Christ, would he have been a member of the circumcision party? Or would he have welcomed the Gentiles to come as they were, as Paul did after his conversion?

So far, we have speculated on our own as if Judah Ben-Hur were a real historical figure. But of course there is one person whom we may regard, more than any other, as an expert on the subject. That is Lew Wallace, who created the character of Judah Ben-Hur and followed him through his many adventures. Wallace had a definite idea of what happened to Judah.

It's five years since the end of the story in the movie. Judah is living with his wife, Esther, in Antioch when a messenger comes to let him know that Sheik Ilderim has left him his palace in Antioch. In the book, Judah's father-in-law, Simonides, is still alive—and, along with the rest of the family, a faithful follower of the Christ.

"Son of Hur," he said, gravely, "the Lord has been good to you in these later years. You have much to be thankful for. Is it not time to decide finally the meaning of the gift of the great fortune now all in your hand, and growing?"

"I decided that long ago. The fortune was meant for the service of the Giver; not a part, Simonides, but all of it. The question with me has been, How can I make it most useful in his cause? And of that tell me, I pray you."

Simonides answered,

"The great sums you have given to the Church here in Antioch, I am witness to. Now, instantly almost with this gift of the generous sheik's, comes the news of the persecution of the brethren in Rome. It is the opening of a new field. The light must not go out in the capital."

"Tell me how I can keep it alive."

"I will tell you. The Romans, even this Nero, hold two things sacred—I know of no others they so hold—they are the ashes of the dead and all places of burial. If you cannot build temples for the worship of the Lord above ground, then build them below the ground; and to keep them from profanation, carry to them the bodies of all who die in the faith."

Ben-Hur arose excitedly.

"It is a great idea," he said. "I will not wait to begin it. Time forbids waiting. The ship that brought the news of the suffering of our brethren shall take me to Rome. I will sail to-morrow."

He turned to Malluch.

"Get the ship ready, Malluch, and be thou ready to go with me."

"It is well," said Simonides.

"And thou, Esther, what sayest thou?" asked Ben-Hur.

Esther came to his side, and put her hand on his arm, and answered,

"So wilt thou best serve the Christ. O my husband, let me not hinder, but go with thee and help."

If any of my readers, visiting Rome, will make the short journey to the Catacomb of San Calixto, which is more ancient than that of San Sebastiano, he will see what became of the fortune of Ben-Hur, and give him thanks. Out of that vast tomb Christianity issued to supersede the Caesars.

About the Author

Mike Aquilina

Mike Aquilina is the author of more than forty books on Catholic history, doctrine, and devotion. *The Fathers of the Church* and *The Mass of the Early Christians* are considered standard textbooks in universities and seminaries. Mike's books have been translated into more than a dozen languages, from Spanish and Hungarian to Polish and Braille. *The Grail Code* has appeared in ten languages since its publication in 2006. Mike has co-authored works with Cardinal Donald Wuerl, theologian Scott Hahn, historian James Papandrea, composer John Michael Talbot, and Rock and Roll Hall of Fame artist Dion.

Mike has cohosted nine series on the Eternal Word Television Network and hosted two documentaries on early Christianity. He is a frequent guest on Catholic radio and appears weekly on Sirius Radio's *Sonrise Morning Show*.

In 2011 Mike was a featured presenter of the U.S. Bishops' Leadership Institute. He wrote the United States Conference of Catholic Bishops' theological reflection for Catechetical Sunday in 2011.

Since 2002 Mike has collaborated closely with the St. Paul Center for Biblical Theology, which he has served as an executive and trustee. He is past editor of *New Covenant: A Magazine of Catholic Spirituality* (1996–2002) and *The Pittsburgh Catholic* newspaper (1993–1996). He is also a poet and songwriter whose work has been recorded by Grammy Award–winning artists Dion and Paul Simon.

Mike and his wife, Terri, have been married since 1985 and have six children, who are the subject of his book *Love in the Little Things*.

Books about Early Christianity
by Mike Aquilina

The Fathers of the Church: An Introduction to the First Christian Teachers

The Mass of the Early Christians

The Witness of Early Christian Women: Mothers of the Church

Roots of the Faith: From the Church Fathers to You

A Year with the Church Fathers: Patristic Wisdom for Daily Living

Signs and Mysteries: Revealing Ancient Christian Symbols

The Fathers of the Church Bible

Faith of Our Fathers: Why the Early Christians Still Matter and Always Will

The Way of the Fathers: Praying with the Early Christians

The Mass: The Glory, the Mystery, the Tradition (with Cardinal Donald Wuerl)

Living the Mysteries: A Guide for Unfinished Christians (with Scott Hahn)

The Doubter's Novena: Nine Steps to Trust with the Apostle Thomas (with Christopher Bailey)

Praying the Psalms with the Early Christians (with Christopher Bailey)

The Holy Land: A Guide for Pilgrims (with Father David Halaiko)

Saint Monica and the Power of Persistent Prayer (with Mark W. Sullivan)

The Ancient Path: Old Lessons from the Church Fathers for a New Life Today (with John Michael Talbot)

Sophia Institute

Sophia Institute is a nonprofit institution that seeks to nurture the spiritual, moral, and cultural life of souls and to spread the Gospel of Christ in conformity with the authentic teachings of the Roman Catholic Church.

Sophia Institute Press fulfills this mission by offering translations, reprints, and new publications that afford readers a rich source of the enduring wisdom of mankind.

Sophia Institute also operates two popular online Catholic resources: CrisisMagazine.com and CatholicExchange.com.

Crisis Magazine provides insightful cultural analysis that arms readers with the arguments necessary for navigating the ideological and theological minefields of the day. *Catholic Exchange* provides world news from a Catholic perspective as well as daily devotionals and articles that will help you to grow in holiness and live a life consistent with the teachings of the Church.

In 2013, Sophia Institute launched Sophia Institute for Teachers to renew and rebuild Catholic culture through service to Catholic education. With the goal of nurturing the spiritual, moral, and cultural life of souls, and an abiding respect for the role and work of teachers, we strive to provide materials and programs that are at once enlightening to the mind and ennobling to the heart; faithful and complete, as well as useful and practical.

Sophia Institute gratefully recognizes the Solidarity Association for preserving and encouraging the growth of our apostolate over the course of many years. Without their generous and timely support, this book would not be in your hands.

www.SophiaInstitute.com
www.CatholicExchange.com
www.CrisisMagazine.com
www.SophiaInstituteforTeachers.org